The Children's Media Yearbook 2013

Edited by Lynn Whitaker

THE CHILDREN'S MEDIA FOUNDATION

The Children's Media Foundation
P.O. Box 56614
London W13 0XS
info@thechildrensmediafoundation.org

First published 2013

ISBN 978-0-9575518-0-0   Paperback
ISBN 978-0-9575518-1-7   E-Book

Book design by Craig Taylor
Cover illustration by Nick Mackie
Opposite page illustration by Matthias Hoegg for Beakus

The publisher wishes to acknowledge financial grant from The Writers' Guild of Great Britain.

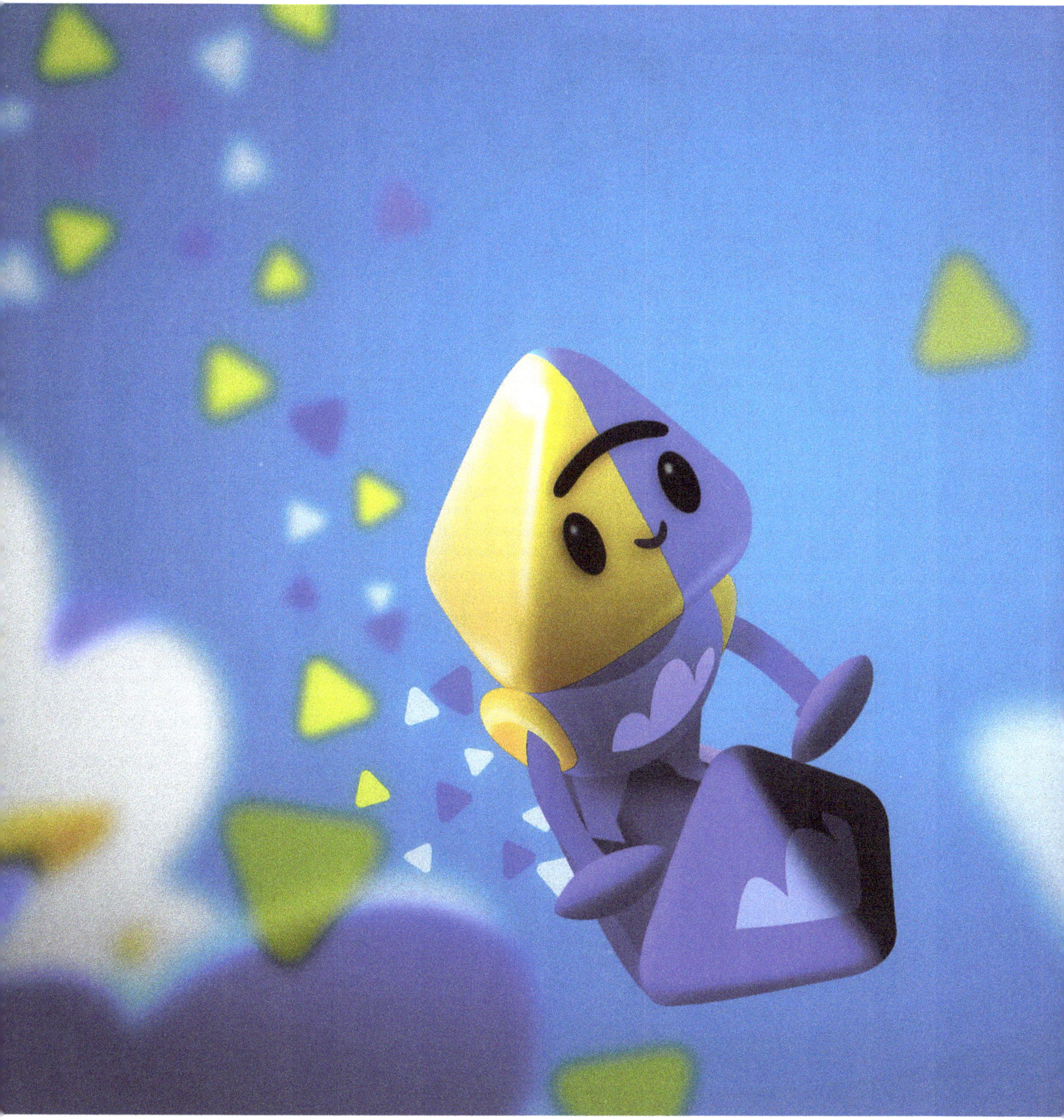

CONTENTS

POLICY, REGULATION AND DEBATE

INTRODUCTION

Editorial 01
Lynn Whitaker

Welcome to this, the inaugural, issue of *The Children's Media Yearbook: 2013*. Published by the Children's Media Foundation, the yearbook provides an overview of the current developments shaping media provision for children in the UK: a snapshot of the policy, production and research issues that characterised 2012 and which remain live in 2013. As an annual publication, the yearbook allows for both reflection on the year past and speculation on the months ahead and, year on year, it will be a useful document by which to track issues and developments as they play out over the longer term. As no other publication of this nature exists in the UK, it is an ambitious enterprise that the Children's Media Foundation hope will become a 'must have' resource for those interested in children's media. Both Greg Childs and Anna Home offer their perspectives on the role and function of the Children's Media Foundation in this introductory section.

However, what a parent, a child, an academic, a policy maker or an industry person considers to be of interest or an 'issue' might be very different and so the yearbook seeks to both represent and engage a plurality of voices, including those of children themselves. And my own appointment, as *independent* editor, reflects an aspiration to look beyond entrenched viewpoints or partisan positions, with free rein given to my commissioning, selection and editing processes. In this way too, the range of opinions here cannot be treated as that of the publisher (or editor) but instead accords with the desire of the Children's Media Foundation to stimulate and sustain quality debate not only in the existing cohort of interested parties and known stakeholders but in wider society too. It is envisaged that, together with each successive issue, the yearbook will function as a historical document by which to map change in the evolving social context or cultural zeitgeist.

Certainly that context has been a turbulent one in recent years, particularly for broadcasting, and I do wish that the yearbook had been in existence several years earlier in order to have tracked the palpable mood of pessimism (and even despair) that – to an outsider at least – seemed to characterise the independent production sector when I first started researching this field in 2006, and which, seven years later, now appears to be dissipated somewhat. 2012/13 would seem to be a particularly significant period for the yearbook contributors, and indeed the overall mood evidenced by many of the industry-related articles in this yearbook is buoyant: quiet confidence that there will be continuing demand, from both domestic and international broadcasters and content distributors, for quality content of UK origination; and a cautious hope that the industry infrastructure can support that demand despite the challenges of a converging - and inherently global - digital media landscape. In no small measure would this faith appear to be predicated on producers' and (for want of a better word) broadcasters' measure of their own role and commitment in providing quality media content for UK children.

The first section of the book, then, presents a selection of 'Industry news and views', with contributions from Joe Godwin and Sioned Wyn Roberts representing children's public service broadcasting from different angles and two complementary pieces from Michael Carrington and Pete Flamman at Turner Kids representing the commercial sector. Turner was my commercial contributor of choice this year (in what will be a rolling selection) and I think those pieces are important in stressing that children's broadcasting now forms part of a global as well as domestic media infrastructure. It seems to me, in hindsight at least, that, back in the aforementioned 'dark days' that followed the effective collapse of CITV in 2006, rather too much was made of how the 'cosy duopoly' of BBC and ITV's terrestrial children's broadcasting might be restored (by fiscal and other policy measures) on a domestic level; and not enough made of how the industry might be better supported as part of a global ecology of children's media. This is why I think Melanie Stokes's contribution on behalf of Kindle Entertainment is also a very important one, painting, as it does, a picture of the reality of a UK independent producer operating in both UK and international markets – successfully - with a predominantly live-action drama portfolio. It is an honest yet inspiring portrait which gives a sense of the passion and commitment required.

In that vein, all of the above 'TV' views share both a strong sense of *specialism* in children's content (a recurring theme of my research with children's content producers and broadcasters) and an insight into what is now a baseline understanding that 'TV' content and channels will have multiplatform iterations as appropriate to the brand. Beth Hewitt's piece – on the one of a kind Master's course in children's digital media production that she runs at University of Salford – further underlines those two aspects while implicitly pointing to the skills and training issues of the sector and how collaboration between industry and academia might present an effective model in that respect. The final piece in the industry section also outlines collaborative approaches and presents the news and views in the games sector: Jo Twist (Ukie) rounds up a rollercoaster year of far-reaching change in the games industry impacting on both consumers and producers. I do hope that Ukie will be a yearly contributor as the very fast pace of change in this sector – new economic models, tax breaks, mobile and tablet apps, collaborations with broadcasters etc. – will be fascinating to chart on a year on year basis.

The next main section of the yearbook deals with the big beast that is 'Policy, regulation and debate'. The section is bookended by individual position pieces from two of the foremost academics in the field. Máire Messenger Davies starts, and was tasked with using the Jimmy Savile case as a means of unpacking some of the issues pertinent to the role of children in television programmes; in so doing she makes a convincing argument for dedicated children's content as a 'right' of the child. Although very different in tone, Jayne Kirkham also adopts a rights-based approach in her account of the wide-ranging activities of the All Party Parliamentary Group for Children's Media and the Arts, and paves the way for the big news story covered by both Oli Hyatt (Animation UK) and Tony Collingwood (PACT Children's Committee) as they outline, respectively, the successful campaign to achieve policy intervention for the UK animation industry, and what that intervention actually means. I am delighted that the yearbook can document that success and, as a policy researcher, I am particularly interested by the fact that the intervention operates in respect of skills and training *as well as* production incentives, given that, more often, creative industries policy is focused only on production. Again, I hope to see the development of this 'story' in future issues of the yearbook.

No discussion of policy and regulation could be complete without contribution from Ofcom and the piece here not only comprehensively sets out the statutory role but also incorporates an overview of the many Ofcom activities in the 2012/13 period, including the latest research into children and parents' media use and attitudes. As many of our contributors make reference to that research it is particularly useful to have an institutionally authored piece direct from Ofcom.

The final piece in the section is from the internationally eminent academic, David Buckingham. He contributes a reflexive and thought-provoking position piece on the ways in which academic research is often misused or misrepresented in respect of 'children and media', to the detriment of public understanding of the terms of the debate.

The third and final main section covers 'Research highlights' from academia and is helpful in bringing the voice of the child to the fore in many of its articles. Acting as a bridge from the David Buckingham article of the previous section, Becky Parry presents a position piece arguing for a redefinition of 'literacies' to better afford UK children a participatory media culture, and drawing on her own research with children as filmmakers. Then, John Potter, in his contribution, argues for no less than a "manifesto for media education" that takes into account children's experience of media both at home and at school: Potter offers some powerful points of evidence from his many research projects. Where Parry and Potter draw on the experience of school-aged children, Cary Bazalgette points instead to her ongoing research with preschool children in order to move the terms of the debate away from that of benefits or harm to a more nuanced understanding of the role of media – and the acquisition of associated literacies – for the very young audience.

Similarly, Lydia Plowman's research with preschool children, across a range of research projects in education studies, focuses on digital media as learning tools and explodes some of the myths concerning children's interactions with digital media. Jeanette Steemers also uses the preschool audience as a research lens but very much in the sense of that audience as a specific market or commodity, as she outlines the particular global and domestic economic forces that shape the provision of television content for preschoolers.

The final contribution in the research section comes from Alexandra Swann, who gives a précis of the UK findings of a large scale international audience study conducted by IZI (the International Central Institute for Youth and Educational Television). Once again the findings and the context of this study underline that the current children's media landscape is shaped by both global and domestic forces.

Following the three main sections of commentary is a final section, 'Farewell', which contains obituaries of the leading lights of children's media - both on and off screen - who have died in the twelve month period preceding publication. It is part of the 'documentary' function of the yearbook that these obituaries will be commissioned or reprinted as necessary and I offer especial thanks to those who so generously honour their colleagues, friends and family with these contributions. I also thank the illustrators and artists who, cover to cover, have contributed the striking visual imagery which helps the yearbook to be so much more eloquent than a collection of prose pieces could be. You will find biographies of all the contributors – who each gave their content for free - at the back of the yearbook.

Plans are already underway for the 2014 issue and I am happy to consider suggestions or submissions of material for any of the sections – or indeed for new areas of coverage. I am already looking forward to next year.

The Children's Media Foundation 02
A new organisation dedicated to the pursuit of the very best media for UK kids.
Greg Childs

Just over a year ago, in winter 2011, the idea of the Children's Media Foundation (CMF to its friends) was born at a meeting of the Save Kids' TV campaign group.

Save Kids' TV, founded in 2006 as a reaction to the disastrous decline in commissioning-spend amongst UK broadcasters, was essentially a single-issue campaign. While UK kids' TV isn't exactly 'saved' (no-one has yet come up with the £35 million of commissioning spend that's needed), it is in some ways in a healthier state than it was in 2006. The main improvement has been in perception. If Save Kids' TV did nothing else, it built an awareness in the press and – importantly – amongst politicians, that there are important issues in ensuring the continuance of quality, range and plurality in UK children's media; that there are dangers in allowing 'the market to provide'; that kids who don't see themselves, hear their own voices and experience their own stories are likely to be disengaged as future citizens; and that the great heritage of successful UK-produced children's content is likely to be lost.

What also became apparent during the five year campaign was that there are many more issues than the economics of television which affect the children's media landscape, and some of these are causes of real concern to parents – and in turn to policy makers and politicians. But so often the debate around these issues is misinformed. There seemed, therefore, a need for an organisation that offered clear and honest research and which encouraged parents, the press and the political sphere to explore the issues more than superficially; an organisation that supported media literacy initiatives amongst children and families to assist that aim, and which continued the campaign for quality and variety across all the platforms on which kids access media, and in the many forms that media takes.

At the same time, the long-established Children's Film and Television Foundation (formerly the Children's Film Foundation) was looking for a new role in the world of contemporary children's media. The CFF made Saturday morning and schools' movies in the 1950s and '60s. This was financed by the Eady Levy, a small tax on cinema tickets designed to temper the tidal wave of US movies flooding the picture houses of postwar Britain – an early example of public intervention in kids' popular culture.

In winter 2011, Save Kids' TV and the CFTF agreed to come together to form a new organisation capitalising on the skills and experience of both bodies.

So what does the CMF *do*? What is it and what does it stand for? Our Chair, Anna Home, outlines the CMF's actions and activities in the first year of its life, in the next article in this Children's Media Yearbook. In fact, this yearbook – the inaugural issue of what will be an annual publication – is a fitting symbol of the scope and interests of the new organisation, with a wide variety of articles from the many different constituencies and personalities who support our aims.

The CMF is not an industry body. Our funding comes entirely from donations by individual supporters. But we are close to the children's media industry and see our role as supporting them in their efforts to offer the best possible media choices for UK kids. One of our Founder Patrons, Philip Pullman, expressed straightforwardly what underlies our aims, when he said that "children deserve the best of everything". For the CMF that "best" is about supporting quality media experiences for UK children. We aspire to represent the young audience – the users and consumers of kids content – on all platforms, whether it be conventional television, films, audio, internet services, games, apps or social media, and we aim to ensure that the environment in which this content is made and distributed in the UK allows it to be the very best it can be.

What this means is that we work closely with the media industry, and equally closely with its regulators; with the academic and commercial research communities; media literacy experts; children's welfare organisations and policymakers, to ensure that content *and* policy are devised using principles gleaned from the very highest quality research. We also draw these somewhat divergent communities together, to help them pursue the best interests of the children they serve and to help ensure a holistic view.

Over time we envisage that CMF will become the accepted 'voice of reason' in the children's media debate. We want to develop a more reasoned and measured public discourse around children's interaction with media. We believe discussion should be informed by an understanding that quality media – and particularly dedicated children's media – can bring enormous value to children's lives: media choices which stimulate, challenge, entertain and inform need to be celebrated and encouraged (by public financial stimuli if necessary).

Building relationships in the research community is a major element in this. We aim to produce a database of existing research which can be used by parents, producers, the press and politicians when they consider what's right for kids. We also plan to identify areas where new research is needed and to partner with commercial, academic and regulatory organisations to make it happen. We aim to keep close to policymakers through our All Party Parliamentary Group (see Jayne Kirkham's article) and our lobbying, so that research-led insight will help the government serve the best interests of the children's audience, rather than serve short-term political gain.

And the campaigns will continue. Our criterion will always be "What's best for UK kids?" Where the market fails them, where regulation is inadequate, or policy misguided, we will act as the voice of the audience to demand better. We will support others as they campaign, whenever it seems to us that the children's audience will benefit, and we will instigate campaigns of our own when needed.

We will work closely with media educationalists to improve the literacy of parents and children. We will also support the archive of children's media in the UK, using the strengths of the past to demonstrate how things could be and should be. In all this, we will be future-focused, taking the long-view of what media means, how the ways in which children interact with it are changing, and the implications of that for them as individuals and for society as a whole.

Illustration by Nick Mackie

We trust that you will enjoy this yearbook, and find it stimulating. It represents an eclectic view of the milestones, conversations and thinking about children and media throughout 2012 and on into 2013. It will be the first of many, as the Children's Media Foundation settles into its role of creating the world's best informed, best supported and best regulated children's media landscape right here in the UK in the years ahead.

The Children's Media Foundation 03
Year One
Anna Home

CMF's first year has involved a lot of thinking, and maybe slightly less doing than we would have liked.

Much of the time has been spent refining our objectives, sorting out our structure and deciding how we will operate, going forward.

We have welcomed out first Founder Patrons, for whose support we are hugely grateful. They already very much represent the range of experience and opinion we aim to accommodate amongst our supporters. Philip Pullman, Anne Wood, Russell T. Davies and Ant and Dec all represent the highest achievements in their chosen fields. Their recognition of the importance of the work the CMF is undertaking is a tremendous boost.

We have created and appointed two part time salaried posts: Greg Childs as Director and Jacqui Wells as Administrator. We have also set up an Executive Committee, comprising of the chairs of a number of our volunteer working groups. They are responsible for concentrating on specific areas of activity, and they recommend policy and action to the main board; other groups can be added as and when they are needed.

Archive	Lewis Rudd
Arts, Culture and Education	Jocelyn Stevenson
Campaign Liaison	Martin Franks
Communications	Anthony Utley
Events	Will Brenton
Internet/Interactive	Marc Goodchild
Policy	Mark Pallis
Political Liaison	Jayne Kirkham
Research & Media Literacy	Colin Ward /Becky Parry

We have also been consulting with a wide range of organisations concerned with children and their relationship with media, including the NSPCC and Childline, the Mothers' Union and various parent groups.

We see one of our main roles as acting as a hub for the exchange and dissemination – to the widest possible constituency – of information concerning children and their media.

2012 Activities

The All Party Parliamentary Group set up by CMF now has 80 members and has met several times, chaired by Baroness Benjamin. Subjects covered have included the animation tax break campaign, and the status of the Bailey Review a year after its recommendations were made (for a full report see Jayne Kirkham's article in the Policy, regulation and debate section).

CMF has contributed to a number of public consultations including the BFI review of the future of film (and its precursor – the Smith Review), where we argued for the importance of films for children as well as families. With this in mind, we have had meetings with Ben Roberts, the new Director of the Lottery Film Fund at the BFI. CMF contributed to the Culture, Media and Sport Parliamentary Select Committee annual review of the Channel 4 licence and drafted questions for the hearing. We also contributed to the Committee's Enquiry on the Creative Industries and to consultations on Media Plurality at Ofcom. Details of all our responses can be found at: http://www.thechildrensmediafoundation.org/action

We also supported the Animation UK campaign and are delighted at the positive outcome (See articles by Oli Hyatt and Tony Collingwood), although we are concerned that this on its own does not solve the problem of the under-funding of children's content in the UK, so the lobbying and campaigning needs to continue if kids are not to be short-changed.

CMF representatives have been frequently involved in public debate on children's media issues in newspaper and magazine articles, radio and TV appearances, and attendance at some key Westminster political liaison events and the Party Conferences.

As we consolidate our position and move forward in the year ahead, there are plenty of issues of concern on the horizon, including the scheduled Communications Act; the ongoing problem of funding for quality UK content; the lack of provision for older children; the future of the BBC as cuts take effect; and regulation of the internet. Others are certain to emerge.

To continue and extend our activities we need financial support. The CMF's finances are dependent almost entirely on the donations of our supporters and patrons. There are a number of ways you can support listed on our web site: http://www.thechildrensmediafoundation.org/my-membership-options-page

We hope that you will feel what we are doing is valuable and worth your support.

In all our activities we aim to serve the best interests of the audience – i.e. children and young people. We want to ensure that the media world in which they are growing up is safe, responsible, creative and fun.

Illustration by The Brothers McLeod

BBC Children's
Joe Godwin

Looking back, 2012 was quite a year for BBC Children's – a significant year in the long history of the Children's service, and definitely a year to remember.

When I was invited to write something for this inaugural yearbook, it was hard to know where to start. At the end of 2011, BBC Children's said a final goodbye to the East Tower at Television Centre, which closed its doors for the last time. It marked the end of an era, but we've already settled into our new home at MediaCityUK in Salford and have now been making content here for over a year.

New shows such as *Wolfblood*, *Wizards vs Aliens*, *Get Well Soon*, *Tree Fu Tom*, *Woolly & Tig* and countless others, have continued the BBC's 90 year old tradition of making their mark on children's minds.

2012 saw the final daily Children's slots on BBC One and BBC Two. From January 2013, most of our content will be exclusively available on our digital channels and websites.

It's definitely an exciting and challenging time for us. Being based at MediaCityUK, Salford has clearly helped us connect more with audiences in the North of England, as well as across the country. We're getting out and about to give children the opportunity to interact with our brands and get involved.

We're also working closely with the independent sector, both in the North and across the UK, with 45% of content last year produced by independent companies. We're forging new partnerships and finding new creative talent both on and off screen.

State of the nation

Children's content remains one of the BBC's key editorial priorities and we're still investing over £100 million a year in high quality, British-made content for children. Producing original UK content is what sets us apart from other commercial broadcasters in our privileged position as a Public Service Broadcaster. About three quarters of everything on CBeebies and CBBC is produced in the UK.

Our mission is to provide unforgettable content to inspire all children across the UK and it remains vitally important to us to give children a voice. Our aim is for every child to be able to see a life a bit like their own reflected somewhere in our content, regardless of gender, ethnicity, ability, family circumstance or where they live.

I want our content to inspire children to think or do things differently and to be active citizens. I believe what we produce can help improve children's lives, shape their outlook and provide memories that stay with them forever. It can make a difference.

Our audience figures show that even with a choice of more than 30 children's channels, plus a million other things to do and look at, audiences are still choosing to watch content that challenges and inspires them as well as just being about having fun.

The success of inclusive shows like CBeebies favourite, *Something Special* (featuring children with special needs), and new animation *Tree Fu Tom* (designed to help children with dyspraxia), is something I'm really proud of. We've also pushed boundaries and raised debate with programmes like *Rastamouse* and *Get Well Soon*.

On CBBC the *My Life* documentary strand has tackled various topics from kidney transplants to alopecia. We've also produced *Newsround* specials on subjects like domestic violence, alcoholism and autism. We're committed to informing children about the world around them, and CBBC is the only children's channel to commit to a minimum of 550 hours of factual programming and 85 hours of news programming every year.

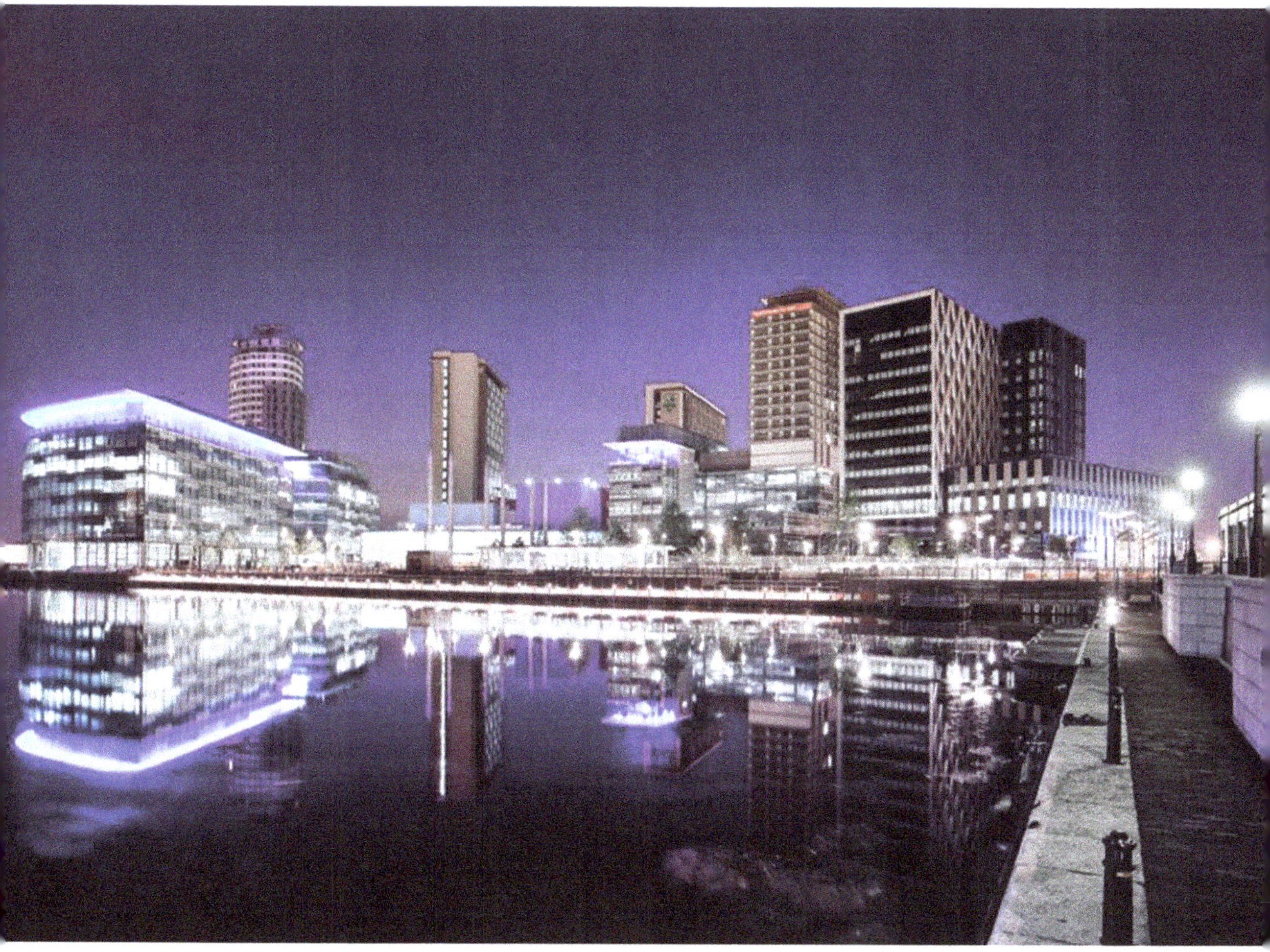

Vital statistics

CBeebies is the undisputed favourite channel in the UK for the under sixes. Over 2.3 million children tune in each week – that's half the target audience – and the current audience share is an impressive 17.5%. In contrast to most other channels, around 75% of content in CBeebies is live-action rather than animation. The CBeebies website and Grown-ups site are also popular, with 830,000 users each week.

CBBC has the highest overall reach of all children's channels – 38% of UK kids tune in each week – and overall share is at a record level of 13.2%. Around 1.8 million children aged six to twelve watch every week. Over the last twelve months, the CBBC website has also averaged 900,000 weekly unique users.

2012 Milestones

In February we celebrated the tenth birthday of our two digital channels, CBBC and CBeebies. Both have gone from strength to strength since launch, with the audience growing exponentially. As well as celebrating on the channels, we invited the audience to join us at a special day of preview screenings, workshops and activities at MediaCityUK with lots of channel favourites. Thousands of people turned up to celebrate with us and it was a brilliant opportunity to invite our audience to visit our new home.

Also in February, Her Royal Highness, Princess Anne, opened the *Blue Peter* garden at MediaCityUK. This was an important moment for *Blue Peter* and for our move to Salford. The garden had been specially transported from London and reinstalled in the public area at MediaCityUK. Rather than being locked away at Television Centre, any visitors to Salford Quays can now enjoy the sunken garden in all its glory.

2012 was also the 40th anniversary of *Newsround*, the dedicated news programme for children. John Craven returned to the *Newsround* sofa in April for a special edition and the show was recognised with a special achievement award in last year's Children's BAFTAs.

The summer of 2012 was a busy one for the whole country. The Queen's Jubilee emblem was designed by a *Blue Peter* competition winner and the Jubilee celebrations were reflected in our output. We also wanted to give our audience the opportunity to feel part of the Olympics, with dedicated content.

Reaching out to our audiences has been really important this year. *Blue Peter*'s Olympic Torch roadshow, in partnership with BBC Learning, took to the road throughout the build-up to the games. *Newsround* offered young people in Middlesbrough the chance to design their own opening ceremony event that was broadcast live on air in July. And Mr Bloom (of *Mr Bloom's Nursery*) followed this with his "Get set, Grow!" tour of the country for younger audiences.

At the time of writing, we've just received the nominations for this year's Children's BAFTAs, which are a great reflection of the quality and breadth of what our indie and in-house teams do. We're delighted to be nominated in many of the categories, alongside great content from some of our competitors.

As well as being the most-loved channel of the preschool audience, CBeebies continues to be recognised by the industry. CBeebies was named Channel of the Year in the 2012 Freesat awards as well as Best Children's Channel at the *Broadcast* Digital Awards. Other award-winning content this year included *Rastamouse* (*Broadcast* Awards), *Tracy Beaker Returns* and *My Autism & Me* (RTS Awards) and *Justin's House* (Rockies). *Horrible Histories*, produced by Lion/Citrus for CBBC, picked up several gongs, including a British Comedy Award for the second year running – the only children's show to ever be recognised in these awards.

Challenges

This year hasn't been without its challenges either. There have been various announcements about cuts and efficiencies within the BBC, and the wider industry is still struggling in these challenging economic times. We are fortunate to have a healthy budget and have now moved to a rolling commissioning system, with new ideas coming in throughout the year.

The BBC Trust confirmed last year that there will no longer be dedicated slots on BBC One and BBC Two for children's content. As the vast majority of our audience watches our content on the digital channels, I'm confident this won't worry our viewers or affect our reach significantly. However, we don't want licence fee payers without children to forget about our content, or not appreciate the important part CBeebies and CBBC play in the overall value of the licence fee. So we're working closely with our colleagues in BBC Vision to ensure there are opportunities for showcasing content and also signposting our channels with well-placed trails.

We continue to operate in a competitive landscape with over 30 options for our audience on the EPG (electronic programme guide) – plus games consoles, mobiles, social media and more traditional choices. There's been ongoing debate on the positioning of channels on the EPG and, especially now our content is exclusively available on the digital channels, we will continue to lobby for changes to levels of prominence.

One of our ongoing challenges is that, unlike other genres, the people who produce content for children are, by and large, not members of the target audience! It's massively important that we talk to children regularly to find out what they like and what they don't, and ask them what they think of content ideas. They are the most discerning audience and our best critics. We use a combination of traditional quantitative research and supplement it with more qualitative research that looks more closely at our audience, building up a real picture of how children consume our content as well as what it is they are watching or looking at online. This includes regular visits to children in the target age brackets - we go to them and they come to us every week of the year.

Media trends

I read the recent report from Ofcom on media use and attitudes (October 2012) with great interest. They found that television still plays an important role in children's lives, especially amongst young audiences, with live broadcast TV still dominating. So - good news for our channels – once again the 'death of television' has been prematurely exaggerated!

But there is also interesting insights for our web teams too. Children are spending more time online with an incredible one third of three and four year olds going online every week and 6% of this younger group using a tablet. So there are some clear challenges ahead to ensure we are delivering and adapting to our audience's needs.

With the development of our websites, the introduction of games for mobile – look out for the new *Something Special* Tumble Tapp game – and even a foray into social media for CBeebies Grown-ups site, we also need to ensure we have a responsible approach to internet safety for children. Whilst it's important to deliver content on the platforms they are using, providing a safe and secure online environment is crucial.

We're involved in the UKCCIS (UK Council for Child Internet Safety) and have commissioned special content around Safer Internet Day over recent years. This year's *Horrible Histories* sketches were particularly effective and were recognised in the 2012 Nominet awards. They're worth a watch on the CBBC website.

How it all works – BBC Children's

Damian Kavanagh left Children's in May 2012 for a new role at Channel 4 and we have been joined by Cheryl Taylor from BBC Comedy. We're delighted to have Cheryl on the team as the new CBBC Controller. There's another new face in the team too as we welcomed Jackie Myburgh to the Controller of Business role early in 2013.

The CBeebies and CBBC Controllers commission all content for each brand – across TV and online (including audio for CBeebies). 50% of the commissioning slate is guaranteed for in-house departments, 25% is awards to independent production companies and the remaining 25% is open to competition from both parties.

BBC Children's has two channels, three websites (including CBeebies Grown-ups), Red Button, Radio Player and we also provide continuity presentation links that help give our channels their own distinctive character.

Looking ahead to 2013

The biggest change from January 2013 will be broadcasting exclusively on our two digital channels. While we know this is how our audience members prefer to watch our content, our challenge is to ensure that new audiences know where to find us.

Monitoring and adapting to digital developments is another key challenge. We don't just want to keep up with our audience; we want to be one step ahead to provide content on the platforms they want in a timely way. The use of iPlayer by our audience has shown a huge appetite for on-demand content, and I believe connected television will play an important role in the way children interact with our channels. And soon. We have already introduced games and content for use on mobile technology and tablets.

Going forward, I also see more co-productions with external partners for both of our channels, particularly CBeebies. As we make cost efficiencies as a business, we will need to look at commercial opportunities to ensure we can continue to invest in the type of programming that only a public service broadcaster can deliver.

In 2013, the BBC Trust will conduct a Service Licence Review of the BBC's Children's services. Findings from the last review, published in early 2009, gave us some clear objectives and priorities to help shape our strategy. We will be working closely with the Trust and look forward to the report later this year.

BBC Children's Board

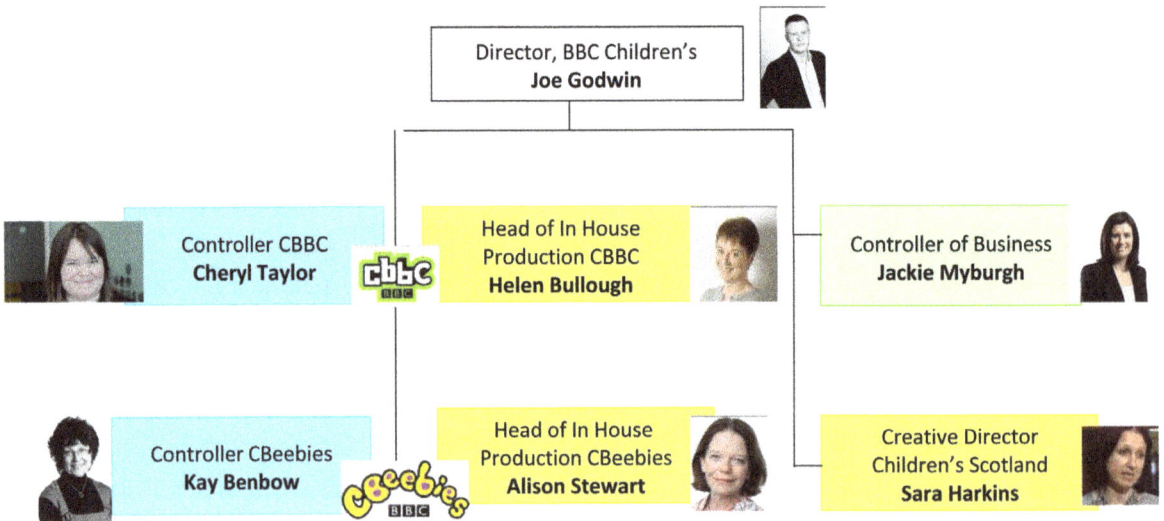

Director, BBC Children's **Joe Godwin**	

Controller CBBC **Cheryl Taylor**	Head of In House Production CBBC **Helen Bullough**	Controller of Business **Jackie Myburgh**
Controller CBeebies **Kay Benbow**	Head of In House Production CBeebies **Alison Stewart**	Creative Director Children's Scotland **Sara Harkins**

UNFORGETTABLE CONTENT TO INSPIRE ALL CHILDREN ACROSS THE UK

Children's Content on S4C 05
Sioned Wyn Roberts

The Welsh Language Channel S4C was set up in 1982 and so has just celebrated its 30th birthday. Back in 1982 there were only four channels, but now hundreds of digital channels are available. Many of them are dedicated children's channels but only one broadcasts in Welsh: S4C. So, in the vast digital landscape of 2013, where does S4C fit in and what lies ahead for the only channel broadcasting children's programmes in Welsh?

Since *SuperTed* was aired on that opening night way back in 1982, children's programming has been at the heart of the channel. In 2008, Cyw, the dedicated preschool brand, and the Stwnsh service for seven to thirteen year olds, were both set up. At the moment S4C can be considered one of the most significant investors in children's programming in the UK after the BBC.

Over the past four years Cyw has grown into a strong and distinctive brand, much loved by children and parents. Cyw (the Welsh word for chick) broadcasts 47 hours of varied programming a week: 8.5 hours every weekday and two hours on Saturday and Sunday mornings.

S4C is hugely committed to providing original, high-quality programmes for young children and their families. Working with creative independent producers in Wales and the UK, S4C has developed the Cyw brand with a slate of imaginative, captivating programmes for preschool and early-years school children. Cyw broadcasts original programmes, co-productions and acquisitions but with imaginative scheduling, so the day-to-day provision on the channel always feels fresh and unexpected. Cyw prides itself on knowing the audience very well and this helps us provide a quality service on screen within extremely tight budgets.

Recent successes include *Dwylo'r Enfys* ("Rainbow Hands": Ceidiog), a brand new series introducing Makaton in Welsh for the first time. Ceidiog also produced the popular documentary strand *Y Diwrnod Mawr* ("My Big Day") shortlisted at the Rose d'Or and Children's BAFTA 2010. *Rapsgaliwn* (Boom Kids) is a hugely charismatic character: a funky bard who raps in verse with the help of his sidekick Dona Direidi. The Christmas episode "Y Raplyfr Coll" is on this year's Kidscreen shortlist. Likeable pirate *Ben Dant* (Boom Kids) hosts a fantasy gameshow on his treasure island. *Marcaroni* (Ceidiog) is a studio-based music show starring West End star, Mark Evans. *Hafod Haul* (Boom Kids) is a farmyard series with talking animals, *Cei Bach* (Sianco) an original drama set in a quirky seaside village.

Co-production is crucial for S4C as a minority language channel and animation favourites on Cyw are *Igam Ogam* (Calon), *Abadas* (Dinamo), and live-action *Bla-Bla-Blewog* ("Ha Ha Hairies": Adastra) shortlisted for BAFTA 2012. Acquisitions range from the hugely popular *Octonots* ("Octonauts") *Peppa Pinc* ("Peppa Pig"), *Sam Tân* ("Fireman Sam") and *Nodi* ("Noddy"), to distinctive indie animation *Siliwen* (Sari): a mix that helps keep the Cyw schedule varied and distinctive.

S4C is a publisher-broadcaster and all the presenter-led links and wraparounds for Cyw and Stwnsh are produced by Boom Kids, an independent production company based in Cardiff. Boom have discovered and mentored new onscreen talent and developed a brand that

From top to bottom Dwylo'r Enfys 1, Rapsgaliwn, Ben Dant, Ditectifs Hanes *this page*

combines live-action with animated characters to create a magical world that children adore. Cyw presenters are much loved by children all over Wales and have a huge following at the many events and shows organised by S4C.

Cyw is broadcast across the UK on S4C on digital satellite television. Cyw can also be viewed online on S4C's on-demand service Clic; 43% of all Clic traffic is for children's content. English subtitles are available on most shows.

Although there are no official BARB figures for preschool children programming, S4C ratings indicate that the monthly reach of Cyw has increased. In 2011-12 the monthly reach was 126,000, up from 94,000 in 2010-11. This is around 47% of the Welsh-speaking target audience.

Cyw also offers digital content tailored to the inquisitive preschool child. The highly distinctive Cyw website cyw.s4c.co.uk/cy is an immersive world with interactive games and activities, and information for parents. In 2011-12, the Cyw website was visited 50,000 times a month and had over one million page impressions; this was up 19% from the same period a year earlier. The interactive website has been nominated at the 2013 Kidscreen Awards in New York. Cyw has been nominated as Best Channel for Children's BAFTA three times.

From top to bottom Igam Ogam, Y Lifft

The Cyw app with stories and songs was launched in November 2010 and has been a resounding success. The app has been downloaded 28,000 times and with the launch of S4C's Digital Fund in August 2012, Cyw's digital slate is ambitious with four new story apps launched in December 2012.

Cyw is not just a television brand; it also has a part to play in the cultural life of Welsh children. According to the Mudiad Meithrin, Welsh Language Nursery Providers, around 60% of the preschoolers come from homes where parents do not speak Welsh, but they want their children to learn the language. Cyw is an important resource for families where Welsh is not the mother tongue as it helps children hear Welsh at home.

Within formal education too, Cyw is a well respected brand and is used in schools all over Wales. A major research project, published in 2009, found that the service played an integral role in the education and language development of preschool and young children. There is a consistent increase in the numbers of primary school children able to speak Welsh and S4C is proud to be able to make a significant contribution to the development of the language.

Cyw gets out and about and stages a number of events and roadshows all over Wales. Every year *Sioe Cyw* ("Cyw's Show") visits the Urdd Eisteddfod, the National Eisteddfod, and The Royal Welsh Agricultural Show and at each event there are around five or six showings a day. *Sioe Nadolig Cyw* ("Cyw's Christmas Show") goes on the road November to January and goes to schools and local communities around Wales. Combined, these shows reached an audience of over 22,000.

Over the last four years, Cyw has become S4C's flagship brand and the next step is to build on that success in the digital space. In September 2012, @tifiacyw was launched, inviting non Welsh-speaking parents to join in the fun. Every morning from 7-8am, non Welsh-speaking parents are invited to watch Cyw with their kids. By following the live twitter feed @tifiacyw (you, me and Cyw) and becoming part of the Social Media group, they will get a user-friendly translation feed during the programmes as well as a chance to contact other parents.

Stwnsh is the strand for children aged seven to thirteen and broadcasts around seven hours a week; one hour every weekday and two hours on a Saturday. The monthly reach of the programmes is 125,000. Stwnsh website regularly has 9,000 visits and 65,000 page impressions per month.

One priority, when I first joined S4C, was to include more comedy and factual content in the mix. There is now a major new comedy series in early development and January 2013 introduced a new documentary series *#Fi* ("#Me": Boom Kids) looking at the lives of extraordinary children. Also in the pipeline is a wildlife strand with an ambitious app. *Tag* and *Stwnsh Sadwrn,* two long-running live shows, are going from strength to strength and the aim now is to build on this with refreshed digital content and strong marketing campaigns.

The Learning slate is new to S4C, and, with creative partnerships, much can be done with limited budgets. *Ditectifs Hanes* ("History Detectives") is a fun factual format looking at the ups and downs of Welsh History. But the commission also included a series of 30 short films to help teachers deliver the History curriculum at Key Stage 2. In collaboration with the Education Department of the Welsh Government, S4C is developing digital content that has lasting educational value. The Government's plans to set up an innovative Welsh Digital Resource (Hwb) for all schools in Wales means that S4C's new learning content and existing archive will be available to all students and teachers.

I joined S4C as Content Commissioner, Childrens and Learning in spring 2012 with over 22 years experience of producing children's and factual content both within the BBC and as an indie. I started in television production but have also worked on interactive projects such as *Colin and Cumberland* for BBC Wales and *Alphablocks* for CBeebies. This shift from traditional television production to digital projects has been invigorating and is now a huge help in developing and commissioning multi-platform content.

The challenge within a multi-channel, multi-platform landscape is to keep the older audience. Once children hit nine or ten, they increasingly look elsewhere. This is true for many broadcasters, but in Wales there's a double-whammy as many young teenagers equate the Welsh language with school and not leisure. And school's not cool. To target young teenagers we are using digital content and second screen technology to try and offer this audience something new, different and sticky that they will come back to again and again.

So for this audience, *Y Lifft* ("The Lift": Boom Kids) the first play-along second screen game for children was launched on S4C in Autumn. By downloading the app, viewers can join in the interactive game and win prizes. Building on this is now a priority and I am looking for interactive, multi-platform content that will offer kids something they can't have on other children's channels yet. *Ben Dant*, a new pirate quiz format for three to six year olds, has just started the first phone-in competition for preschoolers and, judging by the initial reaction, it won't be the last. Being a small broadcaster means we have the freedom to experiment and take risks. And taking risks may well be the only way to reach out to older children.

S4C is unique: it is the only broadcaster of Welsh language content in the world. But that's not enough. We can't take the audience for granted. With so much content available in multi-channel homes we can't expect children to stay loyal to S4C, especially as they get older. The challenge is to create content they crave on all platforms, with limited budgets.

So thirty years on, S4C has come of age and is on the cusp of a new digital phase with exciting possibilities.

Turner Kids' Entertainment 06
Michael Carrington

Picture the scene if you will … It's October 2012 in Cannes, where around 500 top television executives are gathered as usual to peer into the crystal ball that is the international children's media business. This year, however, MIP Junior has a particular resonance for me and for Turner Broadcasting. It's the twentieth anniversary (almost to the month) of Cartoon Network – and not only do I have the honour of being the main host of a celebratory lunch, but Stuart Snyder, who heads up our overall kids' business in the US, has been invited to give the prestigious MIP Junior keynote speech. Turner is in town!

And what an amazing two decades it's been for our flagship channel. In fact, it's quite incredible when you think back to September 1993 and realise that Cartoon Network was actually the very first fully dedicated channel offering children something every day, all day. It was, of course, a time when pay TV was very much in its infancy. Dedicated children's programmes were mostly broadcast via blocks of children's content on the BBC and ITV. And you had to watch what was put out when it was put out - a situation that is totally beyond the comprehension of our young audiences today. Now, Cartoon Network is distributed to over 100 territories in the Europe, Middle East and Africa region (EMEA) and there are about 30 dedicated children's channels in the UK alone. And that's not to mention the immeasurable number of entertainment choices readily available to kids at the click of a mouse …

At Turner, we never, ever, forget that children now have access to a huge range of content wherever and whenever they want it through television, online and mobile devices. So we are constantly adapting and developing our multimedia offerings to ensure we keep stride with the growing expectations of our audiences.

Our latest international hit, *The Amazing World of Gumball,* is a prime example of a show launched with multi-platform touch points. As our first animation produced in

Europe, we had first-hand access to the show's creators and were able to make bespoke and highly engaging content for a range of platforms, including online, social, mobile and gaming. More about the phenomenon that is *Gumball* later, but let me give you just two or three examples of what I'm talking about. *Suburban Karate Master*, an online game based on the series, has achieved over 250 million game plays worldwide. A YouTube video of one of the show's characters dancing ('Banana Joe') has been watched over 2.5 million times. And a mobile app for Android and iOS has been downloaded over 500,000 times. Digital applications were very much at the forefront of our minds when we originally conceived and planned *Gumball* and we were right on the button there; this digital success has reaped huge benefits for both the show and the company in terms of building awareness around the world.

Indeed, our digital offering generally continues to go from strength to strength. Just this year, I'm pleased to report that we had our biggest month ever across Cartoon Network's combined seventeen EMEA websites, with page views up over 100% year on year and fan visits up almost 40%. Engagement levels are high, too, with kids spending an average of twenty minutes interacting with our content.

2012 has also been the year that we've seen mobile move firmly into the mainstream, with over four million downloads of our apps in the first eight months. This is thanks to our focus on delivering an integrated digital strategy that supports our ambition to make Cartoon Network *the* home for kids' entertainment. Games, too, are a big part of the channel's success across all digital platforms. Making even more creative games that use our characters and shows to bring kids together into a fun, shared environment (like online virtual world 'Toonix' launched last year) will be a key part of our plan moving forwards. Community, too, will be another big focus for us, whether it's increasing the ways kids can play and challenge each other, share their enjoyment of our shows, collect and swap content or access exclusive fan content. What's important to us is that they feel part of the Cartoon Network digital community.

Having said that, the channel business remains our primary concern and as our audience base has grown, so our network has evolved. Building on the success we created with

From top to bottom Ben 10, Gumball, Mr Bean

the great library of content acquired from Hanna-Barbera in the early 1990s and (later) Warner Bros, we now commission original productions. As a result, in 2012, Cartoon Network launched new seasons of our recent successes *Adventure Time*, *Regular Show* and *The Amazing World of Gumball*.

Also rolling out this year is *Ben 10: Omniverse*, the latest incarnation of our mega-hit series. This fourth season continues to follow the adventures of Ben Tennyson, bearer of the Omnitrix, a watch-like device that allows Ben to change into aliens. Always attuned to the need to keep our franchises fresh and stand-out, we've given the show an interesting new spin; the episodes alternate between that of eleven year old Ben and fifteen year old Ben as he does battle with a mysterious new enemy.

New series launched by our partners this year include *Star Wars: The Clone Wars*, *The Looney Tunes Show*, *Green Lantern*, and *Transformers Prime*. And I have to mention Cartoon Network US's live-action movie *Level Up*. The success of the movie has inspired a whole series which will launch here in the UK in 2013.

At this point, I hope you'll excuse a little self-indulgence on my part, because *Gumball*, our chaotic blue cartoon cat who has become a global superstar, truly merits a paragraph all of his own. As I write, he has garnered a silverware cabinet of thirteen top global awards (including two BAFTAs) and has an International Emmy in his sights early in 2013. What gives me particular pleasure is that *The Amazing World of Gumball* is a European production – created by a Frenchman, directed by an Englishman and produced in the UK and Germany by a truly pan-European creative team. And the best thing of all, is that children all over the world love watching *Gumball*.

Of course, Cartoon Network is our primary kids channel and is undoubtedly the one that's most well known throughout the entire world. But in EMEA, the region I look after, there are two other channel brands in the Turner portfolio that are equally successful. And they're particularly popular in the UK.

Boomerang, launched here in 2000, is aimed at four to seven year olds and their families. The content on Boomerang is – we hope – fun, entertaining, and exciting, because our intention is to make not only children giggle away, but their parents and care-givers, too.

Many of the shows on Boomerang you'll remember from your own childhood, but more often than not they've been given a modern twist. This year, for example, Boomerang showcased classic programme brands like *Pink Panther, Mr Bean,* and *Garfield* (newly realised through CGI animation), and, building upon our own Hanna-Barbera library, also presented new productions of *Tom and Jerry, Scooby Doo* and *The Batman.*

It's a tribute to these perennial favourites that Boomerang has a unique ability to cross age barriers and offer co-viewing experiences: boys sit down with their dads, youngsters with their older siblings, toddlers with their grandparents. As well as fostering what I think are important bonds within families, the channel acts as a bridge between our preschool audiences and our older kids audiences.

And then there's Cartoonito … We're seeing incredible momentum for our dedicated preschool channel, which premiered in the UK in 2007. Cartoonito's goal is to offer a range of upbeat and quirky programmes that stimulate and inspire young audiences between the ages of three and six. To deliver on this promise, we source the very best of British and acquired programming specifically made for this audience. It's relevant, modern and rarely a passive experience!

If you've never watched Cartoonito, can I urge you to give it a try sometime? It's a channel we're immensely proud of because we think it's very different. Essentially, it's thirteen

hours of brilliant preschool children's TV every day, hosted by six lovable ... well ... shapes, for want of a better description. Known collectively as 'The Cartoonitos', they display all the characteristics of preschool children - and they are just as curious, lively and amazed about the world as their young admirers. And in planning the channel's output, we take care to structure the schedule to cater to the mood of our viewers at different points of the day through our selection of lively, entertaining programmes full of creative, musical and imaginative activities.

With Cartoonito, we take an all-inclusive approach to both boys and girls by providing programmes with broad appeal. Crucially, we aim to reflect the lives of the children watching the channel by commissioning and producing special content for them, much of it from the EU. This year, for example, we launched the live-action series *Ha Ha Hairies* produced by Adastra Creative in Wales, the dynamic CGI series *Jelly Jamm*, from Spanish production company Vodka Capital, and the ever popular *Fireman Sam* from HIT Entertainment.

As we near the end of 2012 we are in post-production on a brand new series of award-winning preschool favourite *LazyTown* for Cartoonito, launching in 2013. As part of its growth strategy, Turner's European division acquired the Icelandic production company behind the show, headed by its charismatic creator and star, Magnus Scheving. Other content for the channel coming up next year is a second season of our popular in-house, UK-produced series, *Cartoonito Tales*, voiced by Jane Horrocks.

As the employee of an American company tasked with writing an article that'll be read primarily by those interested in the British children's media industry, there's one last point I'd like to make that I think is very important. Although the majority of Turner Broadcasting's original production comes through Cartoon Network Studios in Burbank, as a global brand we believe 100% that the only way to make the right connections with our audiences is through embracing stand-out ideas wherever they might come from in the world.

This means that we'll continue to look for creative partners everywhere who are passionate about great storytelling and can come up with unique characters and develop distinctive visual styles for us. Our productions will be mainly animation, but we also welcome compelling live-action concepts for our channels. I think it's true to say that, having just celebrated twenty years of Cartoon Network success and with other channels such as Boomerang and Cartoonito gaining major traction in many territories in Europe and beyond, we're recognised as an innovative leader in the global children's entertainment industry in what is a highly competitive market. After all, we're now available in 130 million homes across EMEA, a figure that, I'm glad to say, continues to rise …

And a view from the business end ... 07

Pete Flamman

When Cartoon Network first launched in EMEA around 20 years ago, any article describing the commercial aspects of the kids' TV business would have been 'Twitter friendly'. Albeit back then it would have been 'Telex friendly'.

When Turner and other international kids' TV players first brought their brands and content to the UK and other international markets the business side of the business was, with hindsight, very simple.

The money to fund the channels (the content, the technology, the staff and so on) came from one of two sources: carriage fees paid by the emerging cable and satellite players, and, to a much smaller degree, from advertising (or sponsorships).

One has to remember that, in the context of UK TV at the time, that was pretty radical: that simply wasn't how kids' TV or content was funded. The key to the kingdom then was the licence fee or a commission from ITV (and, occasionally, Channel 4).

The reality for Cartoon Network (and others like us) was that during those early years we operated at a loss – we were making an investment based upon a vision of a future when kids and their parents would accept and welcome much more choice in terms of what they watched and how, where and when they watched it. That would give us the scale to change from being in the 'import business', based around US content and money, to a situation where we were self-funding, investing in the creation of our own local content *and* also participating in and influencing the global content decisions of our parent company.

I would love to say that everything turned out exactly as we imagined. But that would be a lie. We have always been great when it comes to content and brands but we weren't soothsayers.

That is perhaps a little unfair as a lot did turn out as expected. We got bigger, we started to make a profit, we started to make local, original content and we now make a far bigger financial and creative contribution to our global content slate. And the twin revenue sources that were the foundation of our business in the early days are still, by far, our most important source of income today, thanks to widespread penetration of multi-channel pay TV.

However there are many factors on the commercial side of the kids' media business today that simply were not on our radar back when we launched.

Anyone in the business today knows that investment decisions now have to take in to account a far wider range of factors – licensing and merchandising potential, revenue share from apps, the windowing and sale of content to other broadcasters, subscription fees from on-demand platforms, etc., etc.

Many of those were concepts or revenue streams that existed when we launched. But the idea that they could be large enough to rival our core revenue streams wasn't seriously contemplated. And yet that is the reality for us today.

That diversity of potential revenue streams probably makes kids' broadcasting sound wonderful, awash with a veritable 'jacuzzi of cash'.

The reality is of course that all those commercial options have made a once simple business far more complicated. It is increasingly hard to make forecasts or to get the full picture. For many people that feels like a problem. If there are so many factors to consider, will the small players get squeezed out? Will the big players give up and move on to focus on something simpler and less risky?

At Turner we think not. We welcome the fact that we are part of complex, diverse, interconnected kids' entertainment ecosystem. There is a healthy exchange of content, talent and technology between all the kids' entertainment players be they PSBs,

international channels, indie producers, toy companies, retailers and the newly emerging digital specialists. We all need each other and no one is dominant – with one exception.

Back when we started it was the audience that was in control – if people didn't want our channels we wouldn't get paid: no subscriptions, no ad sales, no nothing. Today that is more true than ever: the viewers (kids and their parents) are in charge and they keep us all on our toes by virtue of their own ever changing tastes and interests.

And that is reflected in Michael Carrington's article. No matter how clever and complicated the commercial side of our business becomes we know that good content decisions are - and will remain - at the heart of everything.

We were the pioneers once and somehow we became part of the 'establishment'. Each year brave new pioneers are tempted to see if they have the right formula to make great content that entertains kids *and* that has a chance of generating more money than it costs to make. If you joined the party this year, welcome. We need you. And we'd love to hear from you.

Looking back on 2012 08
A year at Kindle Entertainment
Melanie Stokes

I start the year at a conference where I am greeted with a sobering fact: over 80% of the globe's kids' TV is produced in the USA and most of it is animation. So, as a British company that specialises in live-action drama (i.e. not cartoons) and has principally served the kids and family audience, I'm not sure a bank manager would totally dig our business plan if Anne Brogan (my co-director) and I were starting out today. But then the TV and film industry has never been driven by such prosaic details as financial viability or P&L (profit and loss). Like many other small indies, we are driven by a passion to make good stuff. Stuff that kids and families will take to their hearts; stuff that will make them think, laugh. Stuff that will hopefully fire their imaginations and make them want to create, play, grow. It's that lofty ideal combined with Anne's legendary Rottweiler tenacity to never let a project go until every avenue has been explored – every broadcaster, distributor, financier chased down and held to account – that has enabled us to survive and pay ourselves and a small team of talented production experts over the last seven years.

During this time, we've had some great successes and some pretty low blows. I've learnt to be less intimidated by middle-aged men with wide girths and both of us have probably got a bit better at withstanding the rejections (of which there are so many that my husband is frequently moved to praise my robustness, making me a) feel a bit better and b) remember that our industry is a particularly volatile one – one minute you're hot, hot, hot, the next you're cold, cold, cold – and that this isn't an especially normal state-of-affairs).

Anyway, I digress, the year starts with this sobering fact. But Anne and I continue to develop ideas we believe might appeal to that 20% left to us. Our second series of *Leonardo* - a steampunk action adventure inspired by the life of the teenage Leonardo da Vinci - is underway, and I spend a very sunny ten days in Cape Town film studios finalising casting and design decisions; discussing the scripts with our rather brilliant young leads (headed by Jonathan Bailey); and making sure the new director (Rob Evans) is not going to totally crack up with the demands of the shoot. Another of our madnesses is that we do like to push our productions to get the best possible looking show for the available money. So, Cape Town gives us some tax breaks and a bigger crew, enabling us to deliver a show that looks as special and awesome as a drama about the world's most sensational thinker, creator and inventor should do. But the director, producer (Lucy Martin), head writer (Pia Ashberry), cast and crew all have to unite behind this desire. And, of course, being as obsessive and driven to be the best as we are, they do.

Whilst there I also hook up with Anne Mensah, the newly appointed Head of Drama at Sky who is also in Cape Town because of two dramas Left Bank are filming there. Sky is very pleased with how well *Treasure Island* has performed (we produced it with Parallel Films) and we're hoping to make a sequel.

Meanwhile, my Anne is off to New York for the annual Kidscreen conference, or "summit" as they call it. This is the biggest gathering of all the international broadcasters and producers who serve the kids audience. It's a frantic five days of pitching, seminars and dinners. The main focus for Anne is our new project *Dinopaws*, a co-development for a new preschool animated series that we hope to get into production by late spring (in fact it takes till late autumn). Anne is meeting our British and Canadian partners and the two broadcasters, CBeebies & Treehouse, YTV. Oh, and we are also up for quite a few Kidscreen Awards – and in fact we win so many for *Leonardo* and a single film we made the year before, *Some Dogs Bite*, that the audience heckles Anne. Back at base camp, Munir, our social-network whizz, tweets Anne's subsequent text to our diehard, unflappable PA, Jacqueline: "So many awards. Bag is too heavy. Will you order me a cab from Heathrow?"

When Anne gets back from New York she is particularly pleased about a very successful meeting with the commissioning editor of CBBC – probably the single most important job in the UK for kids commissioning. But on her return, we discover that he is leaving for a new job at Channel 4. This is a blow. What will it mean for *Leonardo* 3? We have big plans for Leo and his mates. And what will it mean for a particularly challenging but enormously significant series of books we have optioned by Morris Gleitzman that the outgoing commissioner had also expressed interest in? But this game of commissioner musical chairs is just another routine challenge in the life of an indie. Who to woo now? The gossip that surrounds the new appointment dominates the whispering at the BAFTA bar. You have to remember to whisper though because you never know who is listening.

Meanwhile, our new production of *Nicholas Nickleby* for BBC1 daytime is underway. We are making a modern version of the Dickens classic, where the writer, Joy Wilkinson, has rather brilliantly substituted the corrupt boarding school for a corrupt care home and the young abused Smike becomes the old abused Mrs Smike (movingly portrayed by Linda Bassett). We're shooting in Belfast with the help of Northern Ireland Screen. It's the wettest summer on record and we are shooting so many set-ups a day that it's only the supremely calm experience of our producer (Susan Breen) and director

(Dave Innes-Edwards) and a cast led by Adrian Dunbar that keeps the production afloat and with its quality intact. Joy makes a set visit and is particularly impressed by the attention to detail provided by the art department. It's this love and care that can make something really good rather than just ok and it's why I love my job. The collaboration and commitment of a crew working on making a story the very best it can be is deeply satisfying.

The *Leonardo* game, produced by our new media partners, Plug-In, is underway. The game will be free online for UK viewers but available for us to sell elsewhere. It's a race game that test-drives Leonardo's inventions and sees him beating the bad guys. There is also a comic narrative that users can follow. The illustrations are so sumptuous and really capture the facial expressions of our young leads. The challenge of producing a game like this is to make something that is a satisfying game experience but also feels like it belongs to the world of the show. We've successfully produced a BAFTA-winning interactive website for our preschool show, *Big & Small,* with Plug-In before and I'm confident they'll create something outstanding again.

The early summer also sees the second must-attend event – the Children's Media Conference in Sheffield. I've agreed to enter a *Dragons' Den* type competition where I'm pitching a new idea for a family drama to four distributors: the dragons. If they like it, they will option the idea and help us develop it. Our idea is to take *The Famous Five* and update it for the 21st century – so tomboy George is a contemporary girl who falls through a rip in time and ends up in the 1950s, where she has to solve weekly mysteries with the gang and hopefully, eventually, find her way back to 2013. The pitch goes down well. I get some offers – but the distributors want to agree terms that I can't possibly agree to in front of an audience of 200 people. So I turn them down – and it's this turning them down that delights the audience. Producers are so used to agreeing to anything to get their show funded that they get enormous vicarious delight in my saying no. It's rather lovely and I do enjoy it far more than is seemly.

Whilst there, I also meet the new CBBC commissioner – Cheryl Taylor. She's come from BBC Comedy and everyone is buzzing about her appointment.

Back in London, Anne's overseeing a new factual show, *Get Well Soon*, which tackles the issue of what it's like for youngsters to go to the doctors. It's led by a paediatrician, Dr Ranj, and looks at the 30 most common reasons a preschooler might find themselves in the surgery or A&E. When it starts to air in the autumn we are amazed by the attention it receives. It seems that kids are really interested in learning about head lice and the rather catchy theme tune (lyrics by Andy Bernhardt, melody by Sandy Nuttgens) can be heard on children's lips up and down the UK. Munir gets sent clips of children singing it on their trampolines. The producer, David Collier, is delighted, as are we.

Get Well Soon

In October, Anne and I have a place on the PACT indie stand at MIPCOM in Cannes. This is the key market for all TV sales. We are here to support BBC Worldwide sell *Leonardo* and launch the new Leonardo game. We have some particularly positive meetings with a Nordic and a Japanese broadcaster and Al Jazeera. We are also launching *Nick Nickleby* with our distributors, Indigo. Sales for the DVD are looking promising. We're also taking meetings with French and German broadcasters about *The Famous Five* — Blyton remains a bestseller in both countries. And *Get Well Soon* is being launched by our distributor, Cake Entertainment. So it's a singularly busy week with up to twelve meetings a day. Swapping stories with fellow brother-in-arms and indie producer, Billy McQueen, helps keep us sane.

But the Autumn brings some tough news. We don't get one single nomination for the Kids BAFTAs. Not one. And whilst *Nick Nickleby* is a critical success — with coverage on everything from *Points of View* and pleased letters in the *Radio Times* to Maggie Brown singing its praises in the *Guardian* and Mark Lawson running a feature on it on Front Row — its viewing figures are disappointing and it does not win the audience our daytime exec, Gerry Melling, had hoped for. The feeling is that the 2pm transmission was just not the right slot and it needs a later one. So now we wait to see if the BBC will grant it that. It's not our decision; we just have to hope for a good outcome.

And finally *Dinopaws* is officially green lit. Hurrah! 52 episodes that will take most of 2013 and some of 2014 to make. It's a lovely show that we hope kids will want to watch again and again with their mums and dads. The scripting and character and design is underway.

Hopefully 2013 will be as busy and productive as 2012. It's certainly been a full year.

MA in Children's Digital Media Production 09
University of Salford
Beth Hewitt

In the period leading up to BBC Children's moving north, I realised the potential of developing an MA postgraduate taught programme focusing on media content development for children and young people. It was an exciting prospect and one that I had wanted the opportunity to develop for some time. Having worked at Granada ITV, the BBC and then with young people and children at the National Media Museum, Bradford and Urbis, Manchester, I had developed a passion for working with young people and producing content for children and young people.

Now, one year after the University has moved into MediaCityUK, this unique MA in Children's Digital Media Production is in its second year. Working closely with the media industry as a whole, the Masters programme has the support of the BBC Children's department and the BBC's Stepping Out, which works with young people and children, finding out what it is the want to see on their screens, what works for them, and what fails to have that 'x-factor' appeal.

This is a practice-based taught Masters programme and, as such, its remit is to develop the students' understanding of storytelling, narrative structure and characterisation through practice and production. The students have access to the best technologies and the state of the art facilities through the University of Salford building based at MediaCityUK. It is an incredible location and one that absolutely raises the bar and the students' expectations in terms of the work that they can produce. It is an inspirational place to study, with studios, green screen, audio dubbing, edit suites and equipment that match the industry's own facilities. This, plus the fact that each day the students (and staff) are surrounded by media industry professionals working in MediaCityUK, means that they get a really pragmatic and insightful understanding of the environment they are aiming to work within.

This said, within the structure of the programme there is much emphasis placed upon actually working with young people and children, both within the production modules and the research module. Students are asked to gather their findings on the impact of children's content on its target audience: what it is children want to watch, enjoy watching and look to find, through watching children's content, be it via the television screen, the web, radio or live interactive productions.

All these questions and more are relevant, pertinent and very much embedded into the MA in Children's Digital Media Production: how young people see the world; what is important to them; the impact our media has on children and young people; and how rapid changes in technologies are opening up so many possibilities, thereby enhancing children's creativity and imagination and creating a new generation of young consumers of creative content.

Director of BBC Children's, Joe Godwin, and the two controllers of CBBC and CBeebies, have given much support to the MA in Children's Digital Media production with the postgraduate students engaging with BBC Children's department on a number of levels. They have engaged both educationally and practically and this has been hugely beneficial to them.

The following paragraphs are written by Alison Kimberley (MA) who is one of last year's graduates from the course:

> Having completed my Masters in Children's Digital Media Production in September 2012 I have been able to apply my learning to working within the media industry. I gained a thorough knowledge and understanding of developing creative content for children that was second to none. Since finishing the programme I have been working in Manchester for the award winning independent production company, Nine Lives Media. Without the knowledge from this programme I feel I would not have been equipped for my work here.

The teaching was extremely relevant to industry and involved a wide variety of industry professionals working with us throughout the year. The modules were appropriate for industry standards and outside of the teaching there were a great many opportunities for making contacts with media industry people working within Children's production and also for understanding how children's production works.

Through chances to visit the MediaCityUK studios; master classes from art designers, editors, producers, directors and executives; as well as the chance to assist with some children's programming research with Savvy Productions (based in Manchester), my knowledge of this area developed so much over the course of the year. I would highly recommend the course for anyone with an interest in children's media who is looking to pursue a career within this area.

During the second semester of the course, one of the module assignments required each student to research a chosen area working directly with young people and children. This proved to be extremely beneficial in building up our knowledge and understanding of the audience of children's content. Within this module we were provided with opportunities to work with BBC's Stepping Out and to work in a local primary school on a regular weekly basis where we were able to research with a real audience of children's television. This work culminated when I was asked to deliver my research findings at the 'Church and The Media' conference held in October 2012 in Manchester. I was on the panel debating Children and the Media with Joe Godwin (Director of BBC Children's), Phil Chalk, (Executive Producer for TransFactory Media) and Beth Hewitt (Senior Lecturer in Media Practice, University of Salford). It was another invaluable - if a little nerve-racking – experience for me!

I have chosen to include Alison's reflection as it emphasises the achievement of a particular aspiration I maintain for the MA. I very much hope that this Master's programme has validity from both academic *and* media industry perspectives: the BBC, children's media producers, the Children's Media Foundation and the Children's Media Conference (CMC) are all interested in the work of the postgraduate students – both their research findings and their creative content output. The programme attracts international students as well as home students and this, I believe, is one of its strengths and appeals. There are practical and important links with the CMC and this is something that the students benefit from each year.

The vital need to understand children and young people and what it is they want to see on their screens (in their many guises) and the creation of innovative, inspiring and original content for this audience is a major area of concern, importance and focus for many. I very much hope that the MA in Children's Digital Media Production at University of Salford is able to support and add to the huge amount of invaluable work that is already happening within the UK and beyond, with a view to building upon the strong foundations of content creation for the next generation.

A Year of Success at Ukie

Jo Twist

I took up my role as CEO of Ukie – the UK's interactive entertainment trade body - at a time of particular opportunity and challenge for the UK games sector. The work of Ukie can be divided into two main areas, both of which are relevant to issues of quality children's media and its power to enrich lives:

1. Policy and skills development
2. Direct consumer involvement

Looking back over the last year (I took up the role in January 2012) allows me to reflect on the progress made in these two overlapping areas and identify the continuing priorities for 2013. I should say, of course, that *children's* games and interactive content is not the whole picture for the industry but is an area where Ukie, as the representative body for the industry, has a particularly important role to play.

For example we have been promoting the lead consumer safety role that the industry plays to government. This has included producing a consumer safety policy paper, outlining our industry's commitment to parental controls on all main consoles, age ratings and consumer communications. We also continue to be a lead voice at the UK Council for Child Internet Safety (UKCCIS).

PEGI has now been implemented as the sole age rating system for games in the UK and Europe. Our website www.askaboutgames.com is a great place to get information about PEGI and advice to make choosing and playing games a more collaborative and creative experience for families. It covers everything that both parents and children might want to know about parental controls, age ratings and online safety but does so in a way that is engaging and – importantly – based on the experience of real families. It also helps reinforce the message that parents themselves have an important role to play.

Sometimes the press will focus on more mature games and the issues they raise, and so overlook the huge diversity of games that are suitable for everyone, as well as other ways of thinking about children's relationship to games including their potential for creative thinking, problem solving, collaboration and engagement in story, to name but a few. One of the things that we are very keen to promote is a greater understanding of the industry as a sector of the creative economy that children and young people may want to work in. The 2011 *Next Gen Report*, presided over by Ukie board member Ian Livingstone and involving independent research from NESTA and Skillset and e-skills, identified both a skills shortage in the UK interactive entertainment industry and a lack of joined up thinking as to how the school curriculum might address that gap. Of particular concern was that there was not structured computer science teaching in schools, or career pathways for school leavers and graduates to fully engage with the UK's world-class video games and visual effects industries.

Ukie campaigned to improve how children were taught how to create technology and one of the highlights of 2012 was achieving that goal - when Michael Gove announced the reintroduction of computer science to the curriculum and the appropriate training of teachers to deliver it. Coding is a critical skill for our industry alongside other STEM skills of Science, Technology, Engineering and Maths. Early in 2013, computer science became a fourth science as part of the EBacc, which was an incredible achievement for our Next Gen Skills Campaign that brought together cross-industry professionals to lobby government change. But what we actually need is 'STEAM' skills as we must not forget that Art is also vital: be it in design, story, dialogue, music, game play, or effects. To this end we are recruiting a talent development co-ordinator who will specifically liaise with young people – school leavers and graduates – offering careers advice and creating pathways. This, along with revitalising our Games Ambassadors scheme will help to raise the profile of game design, development and production as a viable career choice.

One of the reasons that we need a creative and vibrant workforce is that our industry moves so fast and games are available on many different platforms. The range of platforms and the rapid growth of technology (for instance in cloud streaming games services) means that the development time for games is faster than ever and the business model has changed too. This is creating lots of new start-up businesses that can take advantage of the ability to market and distribute digital games directly to consumers. Very small studios and even student enterprises can compete in the new market for tablet and mobile gaming apps. It's very exciting and there are new developments all the time.

Also exciting – and part of the government's commitment to supporting skills development in the sector – is the introduction of tax breaks for UK games production. Even the smallest of companies or a UK developer working on their own (as a company) will be able to take advantage of these breaks as there is no minimum budget required for the project to qualify. I think we will see developers taking creative risks and trying new things and I am particularly interested to see how the cultural test will shape content because the tax break is there to encourage more distinctive British cultural products.

Where I personally would like to see more development is in collaboration with other content producers for true media convergence in the children's media landscape. Some fantastic collaborations are leading the way as to how we might imagine truly compelling content – *Sesame Street Kinect* for example – but we are only scratching the surface of the creative potential of playful collaboration and I think the interactive potential of 'broadcasting' is set to transform.

Looking back then on 2012 there are three particular achievements that I think are of enormous value to our industry: getting Michael Gove to recognise the importance of computer science skills; PEGI ratings becoming law; and the tax break system for UK games production. Implementing, advising and achieving these changes will make for a very busy and exciting 2013.

Policy,
Regulation
and Debate

Representation and rights 11
The use of children in television programmes
Máire Messenger Davies

The case of Jimmy Savile and his ability to 'groom the nation' and get away with abusing children and young people with impunity for over 30 years, often on broadcasters' own premises, has horrified us all. It raises many questions, most particularly how to safeguard the interests of children taking part in television programmes. Indeed, it raises the question of whether children should be used in programme-making at all.

Not to see real children on television seems unthinkable, and when it comes to children's programmes, 'children's' would surely not be 'children's' if children did not take part. There was a happy reminder of the ways in which children and their lives featured prominently on the main television channels during the recent weekend celebrating 30 years of CITV on the CITV digital channel: *Press Gang*; *Children's Ward*; *The Tomorrow People*; *Art Attack*; *How (To)*; Saturday morning mayhem with Ant and Dec … It was the most sustained weekend of entertaining TV I've seen for a long time, and it was crowded with children: child actors and performers of every age and many 'real' children taking part in the Saturday morning fun.

This weekend – celebrating the lost culture of ITV's original, home-grown children's programming – coincided almost exactly, and poignantly, with the removal of children's programmes from the main BBC1 and 2 channels onto the digital channels, CBeebies and CBBC. 'Children's' programming is now no longer part of the mainstream in broadcasting and it remains to be seen what impact this will have on the provision of resources for original children's production, when adults (and perhaps more importantly, older children and teenagers) no longer come across children's material in the course of their afternoon and evening viewing.

As this CITV nostalgia-fest showed (and as a decreasing amount of original children's production, now mainly confined to BBC Children's, still shows) – in drama, game shows, quizzes, news, and factual programmes – a crucial requirement of a children's programme has traditionally been that it should have some actual kids in it. This raises another perennial question, which the 'ghettoisation' of BBC Children's also raises: what exactly is a children's programme and how is it different from an adult one? What distinguishes a show that should go out on CBBC from one that could go out on BBC1? All the above genres are adult genres too and, as we know, children have always enjoyed many programmes made for adults. Similarly, many programmes for children, particularly comedy, use mainly adult performers – the glorious *Horrible Histories* springs to mind. Indeed, adults making idiots of themselves have long been a staple of children's humour, from Mr Pastry to *Rentaghost* to *My Parents are Aliens*, and long may this continue.

The most useful distinction I've found between children's and adults' and which I've repeatedly quoted, comes from a 1995 article by Cary Bazalgette and Terry Staples. They argue that a children's story is told from the child's point of view, not the adult's: they "foreground [children's] problems of coping with adults or coping without them". This difference in point of view, and in agency, when it is a child or children who are the main protagonist(s) and who drive the story forward, is often what distinguishes a children's programme. In which case, children – whether child actors, or child participants – have to be featured in the programme. The Savile case prompts the question: how can children be protected from adult exploitation in a rather hothouse entertainment world which is primarily dominated by adults working under intensely pressurised and competitive conditions? Children's production is part of this world, so how does the treatment of children used in children's programmes differ from the treatment of children in adults' programmes?

None of these are new questions and I have been quite surprised at the extent to which commentators on the Savile case showed their lack of awareness of earlier discussions of the subject. The producer of Savile's BBC show, *Jim'll Fix It*, Roger Ordish, who worked on the show between 1975 and 1986, said on Channel 4 News on 8th October 2012 that there were no child protection procedures in place at that time (the show ran from 1975 to 1994). This was not the case. There was the law for a start, which not only protected children from assault and abuse, but also protected child performers' working conditions, such as the hours they were allowed to work, and the requirement for chaperones. And in addition to this, there were various internal producer guidelines.

Rules and guidelines

My colleague Nick Mosdell and I reviewed the regulations existing in the 1990s as part of a study on the use of children in adult programmes, which we carried out for the Broadcasting Standards Commission (BSC) (Messenger Davies and Mosdell, 2001). This research was commissioned by the BSC in response to a number of complaints they'd received about children being exploited and distressed in adult programming – a little girl bursting into tears when required to compete in a staring competition on Channel 4's *TFI Friday*, for example, and a child seeking adoption being reduced to tears in a *Panorama* programme.

Our review of the regulations found that both legislation and industry guidelines existed to limit the hours worked by child performers; to protect their health and safety; to provide chaperones and to give them regular educational support so they did not miss out on schooling. Children could only work with licences issued in advance by local authorities. These legislative requirements applied – and still do apply – to the *employment* of children as performers, but not to child participants who were not being paid; they would have applied equally to children in adult and in children's programmes. Where children were used as background members of the audience, as in *Top of the Pops*, or where children featured as themselves, rather than as performers, as happened with *Jim'll Fix It*, the strict legislation on working conditions, health, safety and chaperoning did not apply to the same extent; they were apparently a matter of producers' discretion.

Programmes such as *Jim'll Fix It*, despite sometimes being described as such, were not 'children's' – that is, they were not made by the *children's* department of the BBC, but by the Light Entertainment department. Being produced by one of the main children's departments within both BBC and ITV, or by one of the dedicated children's production companies/channels such as Disney or Nickelodeon, is a useful rule of thumb to define 'children's'. Our research back in 2000-2001 found that non-employed children appearing in children's programming were treated differently – and with greater care – than those in adults' programming. Nevertheless, during the period of our research, there were producer guidelines for both the BBC and ITV which covered the use of non-performing children in adult programming. The BBC Guidelines we consulted in 1999-2000 stated: "The use of children in programmes often requires handling with great care [...] programme-makers must have due regard for the welfare of children who take part in their programmes" (BBC 1999: Chapter 14). More recent BBC Editorial Guidelines (2005) stated that: "In the course of our work, if we suspect a child may be at risk or we are alerted by a young person to a child welfare issue (including allegations against BBC staff) the situation must be referred immediately to the divisional manager with responsibility for the Child Protection Policy" (2005:89). A 2007 Ofcom report on 'Children in Programmes' also took up the theme:

Rule 1.26: Due care must be taken over the physical and emotional welfare and the dignity of people under eighteen who take part or are otherwise involved in programmes. This is irrespective of any consent given by the participant or by a parent, guardian or other person over the age of eighteen in loco parentis.

Rule 1.27: People under eighteen must not be caused unnecessary distress or anxiety by their involvement in programmes or by the broadcast of those programmes (Ofcom/Sherbet Research, 2007).

Producers' views

These guidelines tend to be drawn up with a particular concern for children appearing in adult, or 'family', programmes. They don't draw distinctions between programmes featuring children, and programmes *for* children, although they are obviously expected to apply across the board. However, the research I have done, in collaboration with different colleagues, showed that children's programmes *are* different in their treatment of child participants. In my experience, children's TV producers are usually very aware of the importance of protecting children and making sure that they are happy and safe, not least because they want to get the best work possible out of them. I interviewed many children's producers for some research on children and television drama, published in *Dear BBC* (2001); child welfare, including an awareness of developmental differences in children, was prominent in the way they discussed their work. One of my interviewees, Roger Singleton Turner, producer of children's TV classics such as *The Demon Headmaster* series, has written a book about working with children for BBC Training, *Television and Children* (1994). In it he points out: "Because of the different paces and areas of development in children, groups of people have grown up in the television industry who try to respond to these differences ... drama featuring children, for children, should not be confused with films and programmes with children that are an evocation of childhood made for an adult audience" (1994:8).

In our 2001 BSC research, Nick Mosdell and I did a case study of the Carlton (ITV) game show *Mad for It*, which used a lot of (very noisy) children competing in games with each other, and which had a live audience of children – not a task for the fainthearted. We found that regulatory procedures for ensuring consent, parental approval, safety, enough to eat and drink, involvement of schools, audience feedback, welfare and active enjoyment were explicit, and routinely applied as part of the production process. We recommended in our BSC report that these examples of general good practice in children's programming should be applied in *all* programming. Although Jimmy Savile's alleged abuse took place during many years prior to our research, there certainly would have been examples of good child protection practice within the BBC during his career that could have been followed for the many programmes he worked on involving children.

Children's rights

Hopefully, the Savile case will not be used as an excuse to condemn all those working with children in television – as an academic at a seminar at a prominent School of Education recently did, more or less claiming that abuse of children must have been part of the culture in the entertainment industry for Savile to go unreported for so long. There is some evidence of child performers not having a happy time in adult programming, and the difficulties of some child stars in Hollywood in the past are notorious. But this should not mean that children should be barred from appearing in the media in their own right. Yes, children need to be protected, but yes, they also need to be heard. This is a matter of children's rights.

Article 3 of the UN Convention on the Rights of the Child deals with child protection:

> In all actions concerning children, whether undertaken by public or private social welfare institutions, courts of law, administrative authorities or legislative bodies, the best interests of the child shall be a primary consideration ...

> States Parties shall ensure that the institutions, services and facilities responsible for the care or protection of children shall conform with the standards established by competent authorities, particularly in the areas of safety, health, in the number and suitability of their staff, as well as competent supervision. (UN General Assembly, 1989: 2)

Article 12 sets out the right of the child to be heard: "the child who is capable of forming his or her own views [has] the right to express those views freely in all matters affecting the child, the views of the child being given due weight in accordance with the age and maturity of the child." Article 13 states: "The child shall have the right to freedom of expression; this right shall include freedom to seek, receive and impart information and ideas of all kinds, regardless of frontiers, either orally, in writing or in print, in the form of art, or through any other media of the child's choice." The UN Convention thus acknowledges the right of children to have their own voices heard, and to speak and act for themselves. Children's television is one of the few cultural spaces where this right is routinely exercised.

One problem with 'ghettoising' children's programming into special channels, is that these voices may now only ever be heard by other children – and not by older children and adults who need to be aware of how younger people are feeling. We should never underestimate the importance of the child's independent voice when making the case for dedicated children's programmes.

The role of parents

Some people argue that parents can speak for children. My research, and that of my colleagues, has demonstrated that this isn't always the case. It is not enough for parents to be seen as spokespersons for their children and to be the sole determinants of what should happen to them and this principle is increasingly accepted in family law. Children are quite capable of speaking for themselves. Even quite young children can argue a different case in opposition to their parents, as children in the *Consenting Children* study showed.[1] If this case concerns their own feelings – for example, not wanting to take part in a TV game show despite a parent's urging – should the child's or the parent's preference be heeded by the producers? We argued it should be the child's.

A big question here is 'competence' – when are children old enough to be able to make independent decisions in their own right? This is a tricky one. According to the UN convention, a child is someone under the age of eighteen, but in this country the law varies greatly in terms of what children are allowed to do and at what age – part-time work at thirteen; sexual consent at sixteen, driving at seventeen and so on. Children vary too. Some six year olds are a lot more confident and articulate than some twelve year olds. The BBC has decided – somewhat arbitrarily many people think – that children's programming serves people up to the age of twelve. After that age, it is not clear what you are. Who serves people aged thirteen to fifteen? Again, research shows that this is a very important and distinct age group with opinions of its own, distinct from those of children in primary school, and different from those of adults (Carter et al., 2009).

One of the strengths of children's programming has been that it gives such children a voice of their own. In our research on *Newsround* (Carter et al., 2009), the opportunity to be heard was seen as one of the most important attributes of the programme by many of the children we interviewed. For example:

> I think it's important for us to share our opinions because it's always adults
> who get to talk and they don't care about children, but *Newsround* does.
> (Martina, Coleraine, Northern Ireland, age 11)

... personally, I feel that the views of my age range are generally left out in most news, although they occasionally give examples; [*Newsround* is] a way for me to share my ideas and have them listened to by an adult who is not my parent. For example, politicians generally won't discuss ideas with teens because they aren't trying to reach us and they don't care about our issues. So I think our views and opinions are not passed across to important members of society. (Edward, Bournemouth, age 13)

Children as illustration

Children having their own voice, and being treated with respect as people with views and talents is not the same as children being used as background 'set dressing' or as props in adult entertainment. Through the internet, Facebook and Twitter, as well as the more traditional uses of children in advertising and charity campaigns, images of children are now everywhere; there is also much greater concern nowadays than there was in the past about images of children being manipulated for exploitative purposes – one of the reasons that mainstream media producers often pixilate faces of children who are not specifically featured in a story. One of the most insightful writers on the representation of children in images, Pat Holland, draws attention to the possibilities of exploitation of children and suggests we should always ask: "What is [the image] for? Who is invited to look at it? What has been made of it?" (2004: 191). She was concerned about the way in which child images may be 'read' by adults. She might also have asked: to what extent does the person in the image control the ways in which the image is presented? As I argued in my book, *Children, Media and Culture* (2010): "After all ... the person in the picture is always a real child at a real moment in a real life." This person should have a say in how he or she is represented.

In our final recommendations to the BSC, Nick Mosdell and I proposed that news editors, picture editors and documentary makers should not routinely use images of children to illustrate difficult or emotive issues; where this is done, guidelines about not exploiting sickness and distress should be followed. Children themselves should also be consulted and quoted in stories concerning them (with full consent and, where possible, parental permission). We also recommended that media assumptions about children wanting

Illustration by Nick Mackie

to appear on television, and having the necessary confidence to do so, should be re-examined. From our findings, parents were more enthusiastic about seeing children on television, than children themselves were. This reinforces the importance of children's consent to appear in the media being sought independently of that of their parents. We also drew attention to the good practices prevalent in children's programming and argued that these should be imitated in *all* programming that featured children.

Why should we support the CMF and what has it got to do with children's rights? We should support it because it offers children access to one of the most basic rights of all, as laid out in the UN Convention: "the right to freedom of expression; … the freedom to seek, receive and impart information and ideas of all kinds".

REFERENCES

Carter, C., Messenger Davies, M., Allan, S., Mendes, K., Milani, R. and Wass, L. (2009) *What do children want from the BBC? Children's content and participatory environments in an age of citizen media.* AHRC/BBC, Cardiff University. Online at: http://www.bbc.co.uk/blogs/knowledgeexchange/cardifftwo.pdf

Holland, P. (2004) *Picturing childhood: the myth of the child in popular imagery.* London, New York: I.B. Tauris.

Messenger Davies, M. and Mosdell, N. (2001) *Consenting children? The use of children in non-fiction television programmes.* London: Broadcasting Standards Commission. Online at http://www.ofcom.org.uk/static/archive/bsc/pdfs/research/cchildren.pdf

Messenger Davies, M. (2010) *Children, Media and Culture.* Milton Keynes: Open University Press/McGraw Hill.

Ofcom/Sherbert Research (2007) 'Children in programmes: An independent research report for Ofcom by Sherbert Research', 12th December 2007. Online at http://stakeholders.ofcom.org.uk/binaries/research/tv-research/rpt.pdf

UN General Assembly (1989) Convention on the Rights of the Child, 20 November 1989, United Nations, Treaty Series, vol. 1577, p. 2.

---------- NOTES ---------------------

1. When both children and parents were given some options of appearing in different TV shows, and asked to say whether they would like to be in/would like their children to be in these shows, parents were consistently more enthusiastic about their children appearing than the kids were.

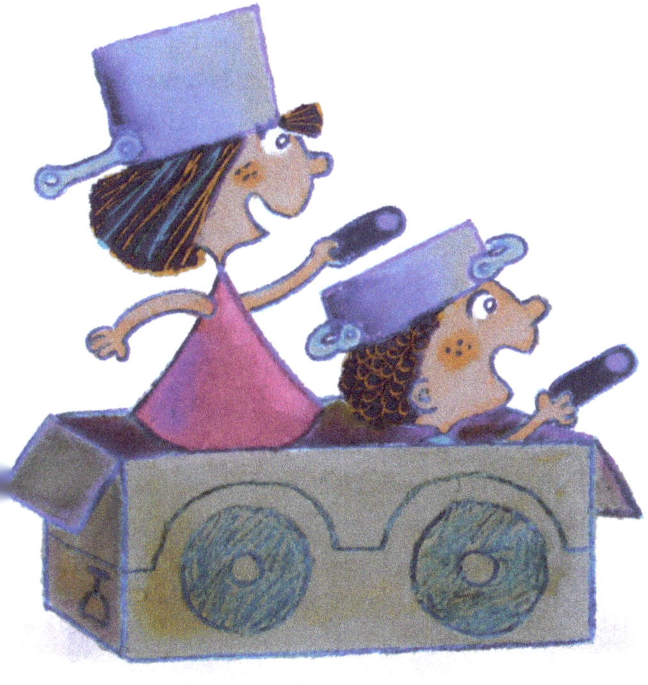

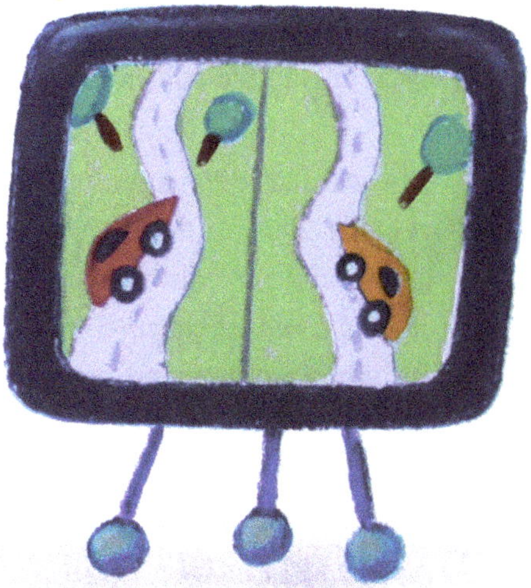

"So what exactly does an 12
All Party Parliamentary Group do?"

Jayne Kirkham

Well, it's a bit like – were you ever in any after school clubs? It's not like that at all. More like the lunch clubs, you know? The ones that no one went to? Yes, but do you remember how the few people that *did* go were the ones the dinner ladies always listened to, saving the best bits of lunch, letting them leave the table early … Yeah that's kind of what an All Party Parliamentary Group is like: not a lot of authority but with clear influence and managing to get a surprising amount done.

The All Party Parliamentary Group (APPG) for Children's Media and the Arts was first registered in June 2011. With Baroness Floella Benjamin newly ennobled and in the Chair, and me volunteering on behalf of the Children's Media Foundation to administer, it was a big adventure into unknown territory. But despite Westminster's reputation for slimy politics and backstabbing, people were helpful and generous with advice and support. Perhaps that is not so surprising, given that everyone subscribes to the idea that children are a good cause to champion. Although, as we know, it is also easy to just pay lip service, pat the children on the head, and then leave them, forgotten, in the corner. But as long as, in both houses of parliament, there are people like Lisa Nandy, Tom Watson and Floella Benjamin (who were the first officers) and Baroness Doreen Massey (who gave tremendous support), then children's issues will not be sidelined.

However, that children's *media* issues will also not be sidelined is, I think, little short of a miracle and thanks largely to the campaigning of organisations such as the Children's Media Foundation. It has been an uphill climb to get parliamentarians to accept that media for children is important, even essential for their development and integration into a mass media world. It shouldn't have been, given that the United Nations Convention on the Rights of the Child states clearly that "children have the right to get information that is important to their health and well-being. Governments should encourage mass media – radio, television, newspapers and internet content sources – to provide information that children can understand and to not promote materials that could harm children" (Article 17), and also that "children have the right to relax and play, and to join in a wide range of cultural, artistic and other recreational activities" (Article 32).

If only I had known about this convention a few years ago. But then I'm just a volunteer who fell into this campaign with no political experience: I didn't even go to any school lunch clubs!

These two articles are at the heart of all that the APPG for Children's Media and the Arts does. The aim of the group is to bring together politicians from both houses and all parties to inform and enlighten them: joining the dots between children's entertainment and education; between the departments of Culture, Media and Sport (CMS), Education, and Business; between children's physical, cultural and social needs; and between kids programming and the democratic process. "Democratic Process?" Um, yes. If children and young people are to engage with the society they are growing up in, then they need to see, experience and understand it. I don't need to tell you how, since the first cave paintings, visual storytelling has taught children how to think and feel and equipped them for adulthood. But there are still people in Westminster who don't get it.

Given how stupidly busy both the House of Commons and House of Lords are, it is difficult to find times when everyone can get together. Nevertheless, and despite inevitable interruptions for votes and other business, the APPG has punched above its weight in 2012. Following the publication of the Bailey Report into the commercialisation and sexualisation of children, David Cameron said he would call together all stakeholders for a six-month review. The six months became seven, became eight, nine, ten ...

Reviews like this have come and gone and little has changed. So while Mr Cameron's date kept slipping and with it the impetus for change, the APPG remained focused and in the end called the stakeholders together for *its own review*. Reg Bailey himself attended and was pleased to hear of the substantial progress the likes of Ofcom, the Advertising Standards Authority and ITV had made in meeting his recommendations. To be fair, Mr Cameron has commissioned Reg Bailey to conduct an eighteen-month reappraisal. But who's to say the powers at 10 Downing St won't be distracted again? The APPG will be watching ...

While meetings are hard to squeeze in, nevertheless the mailing list of interested parliamentarians has grown, as we seek to keep them informed with briefing documents and newsletters about the children's arts and media worlds. When Animation UK were pushing hard for an animation tax break early in 2012, the APPG got right behind the campaign with an event in Westminster timed to give MPs one last push before the budget. Perhaps my proudest moment of that year: taking Wallace and Gromit to Westminster. I got to act out my own plasticine version of *Mr Smith Goes to Washington*! Not just these two but other much loved cartoon characters such as Fifi (of *Flowertots* fame) and Roary the Racing Car (see I'm on first name terms with these A-Listers). There were some security concerns: what if one of the cartoons brought in a cartoon bomb?

The event was a success, resulting in new supporters and letters written to the Chancellor urging him to give the tax break. Which he did. Now, of course, we have to see how and what this break will actually be. It would be naïve to think the war was won, as, at the risk of repeating myself, we all know how easy it is to pay lip service to children's issues and then leave them alone in the corner. While members of the animation industry work with the Treasury on the practicalities of the tax relief, members of the APPG lend political back up.

The summer recess was a good time to take stock of both the APPG and how it can best fulfil its mission statement. The biggest issue is most definitely that of time. Everyone is time poor. So meetings have to be of real value to both parliamentarians and those that seek their help. So rather than have meetings for meetings' sake last autumn, and also to allow for better preparation and research, I decided instead to spend time getting to know individual members, with a view to matching campaigns with their own interests. Well someone had to attend the party conferences.

Party Conferences: bit like MIPCOM but with fewer yachts, less style, but more champagne. Which makes up for the speeches.

Attending the conferences and the subsequent follow up meetings has proved successful, with individual peers and members of the CMS and Education select committees not only giving valuable advice, but picking up the baton and running with a number of issues. For example: holding Channel 4 to account over its 2011 provision for "older children"; highlighting the consequences that the English Baccalaureate, even before it is launched, is having on the arts both in and out of school; maintaining the BBC's commitment to Children's; keeping up the pressure for the Animation Tax Relief; urging more financial support for children's film; and campaigning for Arts Council funding to include more projects for children, to name but a few.

These topics won't just go away. Although sometimes when I'm more jaded and yet again have had a meeting postponed, I think that the best tactic a politician has is to hope that people will simply get fed up and go away. It is tempting, really tempting after a meeting has been rescheduled for the third, fourth or even fifth time and I'm now looking at a date three months hence, to just leave it be. Sometimes it is hard to even remember why I wanted the meeting in the first place. And then I look at the telly.

So 2013 is now upon us and the APPG for Children's Media and the Arts will continue bringing together politicians, industry and audience. Michael Gove's English Baccalaureate is an issue for many. Probably more than yet realise it. The teaching unions are aware of its impact on their members and are seeking to have it done away with altogether. Other trade unions are still making up their minds – do they remain neutral, back abolition, or find a more pragmatic approach? But I wonder if many are really aware of the impact it will have on our young people. I had a rotten experience of the arts in schools but others were inspired to pursue successful careers. If schools do not include the arts in their curricula, then where and when will children have any access to music other than commercial pop; drama other than soaps; art other than graffiti? Mozart is reduced to the ice cream van's jingle, Shakespeare misquoted by American detectives, and Old Masters re-mastered for mouse mats.

There is clearly a debate to be had about who provides the artistic and cultural experiences for children: should it be within the Education system or outside, provided by the great arts organisations? Both are strapped for cash right now and the trouble is, that while adults debate, children grow up. They'll never be eight, or nine, or ten again. They'll never have that same wonder and curiosity. It's easy, while the debate rages, to forget we've, yet again, put the children in the corner.

The same argument needs to be had over at Channel 4. For even though the channel was given a brand new remit (inserted into the 2003 Communications act by the 2010 Digital Economy Act) requiring it to "participate in [...] the making of relevant media content that appeals to the tastes and interests of older children and young adults", it doesn't seem to have gone out of its way to fulfil that new remit. Each public service broadcaster has to report annually to the Culture, Media and Sport select committee. Questions are asked of the report, answers are given and unless anyone makes a fuss, that's an end to it for another year. But the Children's Media Foundation scrutinised Channel 4's 2011 report and submitted its own questions to the APPG members that are also on the select committee. Rather than that being an end to it for another year, Channel 4 is being called to account: the select committee has asked for further evidence from the Children's Media Foundation.

This kind of information flow is surprisingly two-way. The APPG is able to gather information from outside organisations to brief MPs and peers about issues of concern, while parliamentarians are able to advise on navigating parliamentary procedure, who to talk to and, in some instances, what to say. This has led to much more effective and timely submissions to a number of inquiries. Of course the real success can only be measured when the inquiries lead to changes in policy or revisions in law. I am beginning to see both.

Will we see more? I sincerely hope so, and in areas that we have not been able to concentrate on previously. Although the Children's Media Foundation set up the APPG, it included "the Arts" in the title and remit. Just as people in Westminster need to join the dots, so too do we need to recognise that children don't care if they get their stories or their culture from books, fine arts, comics, cartoons, telly, film, that clown in the shopping precinct ... So two of the issues that we will be looking at in the coming year are the British Film Institute's provision for children's film in the UK and also Action For Children's Arts' campaign for better Arts Council funding for children's projects. We are currently researching these areas with a view to bringing together the people that matter and that care enough to bring about change where change is needed.

If you are such a person then I ask you to get involved. At the very least write to your own MP about the children's media and arts issues that concern you. They need your vote and it is their job to listen to you. Tell them about the APPG and get them involved.

Watching out for children's media and arts is a bit like the elephant that needs eating: there's just so much, it's hard to know where to start. And just when you sink your teeth into a nice bit of ear and think that, say, Channel 4 are going to have to do more to fulfil their public service remit to "older children", you hear rumours that the BBC might cut their children's budget after all and you realise that this elephant has another ear and it's flapping wildly. And don't even mention the tail. I don't want to go near the tail. We need other nibblers: people who understand the arguments and are prepared to give up some time and energy to keep on top of the topics. I mean, if I know other people have got the ears, and the feet and the trunk, then I'm willing to take the tail. Has anyone got an umbrella? Don't ask why I would think I would be eating a live elephant. It's probably because I had inadequate cultural and artistic opportunities as a child and my imagination never quite climbed out of the toilet. Or maybe it's because the grown-ups around me were too busy debating far more important things to notice that they had left me alone in the corner.

Illustration by Matthias Hoegg for Beakus

this page

2013 should prove to be an important moment in history for the animation industry as the government announced, in March 2012, that they are going to introduce a tax credit for animated programs. As George Osborne MP put it, "Wallace and Gromit will be staying exactly where they are!" And George was right: if animation does not get the support it needs it will be inevitable that, in the near future, no more productions will be made in the UK.

Osborne's sound bite was a great piece of advertising for our friends at Aardman who, as a household name, played a large part in getting the Animation UK campaign to where we are today. So I'm going to unashamedly use this piece to laud the people that made the campaign a success, because as an industry – and beyond – we need to understand the effort people made to make this possible.

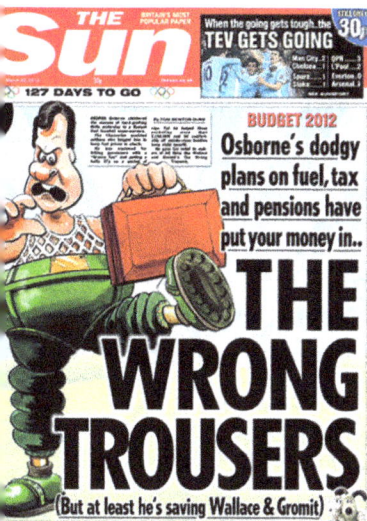

Animation UK was born out of a realisation that our industry was quickly sliding away to nothing: we had lost over half our home-produced animation in a little over five years, and companies that were once the powerhouses of British animation were shutting down, selling up or moving overseas. We could not compete on a level playing field with the rest of the world who were getting a generous range of support mechanisms from their governments. The choice was black or white for HMG: help the industry, or lose the industry. They chose to help.

79

I guess I should start at the very beginning with our Patron and political supporter, Mark Field MP, whom a small number of animation professionals met three years ago. We spent our first meeting talking through the industry, its problems and the solutions. He asked sensible questions and, like all MPs, made sympathetic noises and nodded and shook his head in all the right places: he was personable, likable and professional.

At the end of the meeting Mark promised to look into the issues and do what he could to help us and as he shook our hands and left, we turned to each other and someone uttered the words, "He's really nice, we will never hear from him again!" We all thought the same; our cynical view of politics and the many failed attempts over the years to get help for animation weighed heavily on our minds.

To all our amazement, from day one Mark was, and has continued to be, absolutely true to his word and we received an email the very same day from Julia Dockerill in his team. They had some ideas on ways forward, meetings Mark could organise for us, and whom he could lobby on our behalf. It's worth highlighting that Julia is far from just a political sidekick: she was our main point of contact and a real driving force behind the scenes politically.

They kept the argument alive in the halls of Westminster, as well as in the main hall of the House of Commons, for over three years. Our main campaign can be considered a 'shock and awe' assault on local MPs right round the country, but Mark and Julia were playing out a much steadier and political campaign behind the scenes.

It was, in fact, a meeting that Mark organised that first created the seed idea for creating Animation UK. He managed to get us a meeting with Jeremy Hunt, the then Culture Secretary, and I prepared for this by compiling as much info as I could on the decline of the industry, the problems it was facing and the possible solutions. I grandly called this document "Saving Animation". Jeremy called it "Numbers on the Back of a Fag packet" and told me to come back when we had a proper and detailed analysis!

I'm certain that as he walked away he thought, "That's the last we'll hear about that!" If so then I'm afraid he completely misjudged how pugnacious I am, and as I left Parliament I thought, "I'll get you that analysis: I'll come back and I'll make you do something about it!" Suffice to say, even when we got our numbers and analysis, he failed to meet with me again, but he inspired me that day to set up Animation UK, and we got a promise of a tax break and he got a promotion to health ... so maybe we all got what we wanted!

So we needed better numbers, and, despite having just read *Dummies Guide to Tax*, I was definitely not the man for the job, and I started making enquiries as to how much a proper report would cost. I presented the preliminary findings at an industry meeting and asked everyone if they had the motivation and finance to help get this done. Mark Field's presence added an air of 'political willingness' to the event, and pretty soon we had people offering us funds and support.

The money slowly built until we had enough to fund a large body of work from the perspective of two industry specialists, who, over the following months, would not only supply us with a conclusive in-depth report, but also with some incredibly useful support and insight into political workings and current thinking in Parliament. Though they are very happy to admit it now, they thought at the time that success was an incredible long shot and that the chance of any progress in the short term was impossible!

Our report, entitled "Securing the future of UK animation" by Robert Kenny and Tom Broughton, was funded by the following companies: Parthenon, Target, eOne, HIT, Wish films, Blue-Zoo, Pesky, Aardman, Astley Baker Davies, Baby Cow, Studio Liddell, Chapman, Classic Media, The Foundation, Plastic Milk, Millimages, PACT, Lupus, Calon, Spider Eye, Save Kids TV, Red Kite, Ragdoll, BECTU, Cosgrove Hall, Komixx and Snapper productions.

Many more contributors provided information, data and insight that proved vital in producing such a compelling document. The main thrust of the document was the economics: showing how the industry was slipping away - with most of our work lost overseas over a ten year period - and how a little help now could reap financial rewards in the future. But this was all neatly wrapped in culture, heritage and the idea of providing children with the very best programming possible.

During this period we were trying to raise awareness in parliament through Mark Field and through the House of Lords using the All Party Parliamentary Group for Children's Media and the Arts, set up by Floella Benjamin, with the support also of Jayne Kirkham and the Children's Media Foundation (CMF), chaired by Anna Home, OBE.

They hosted a number of discussions as well as allowing us to turn the House of Lords in to a temporary animation exhibition, shortly before the Budget.

Greg Childs from the Children's Media Conference also allowed us to meet and talk at their events, as did BAFTA.

As well as a political presence we needed to have a public-facing campaign, or, as one senior MP told me, "Get Mumsnet behind it and it will happen, they run the country now!" We used PR Company Parys Communications, who were generously funded by Blue-Zoo, but who also did a huge amount of work for nothing.

House of Lords exhibition
this page

They got us several BBC appearances on TV and Radio and many articles in the industry press, including *Broadcast*, which became such a huge backer of the campaign they even let us take over the front page one week!

Broadcast

Backing
ANIMATION UK
tax break campaign

www.broadcastnow.co.uk   16 March 2012

C4 sets May deadline to revamp entertainment

Disney: tax breaks would lure us back

We struggled, however, to cut through to the national papers, but that all changed thanks to Aardman and in particular Miles Bullough. Being the biggest and most public-facing company, they agreed to speak out and the interest they generated – in a series of articles about them "possibly" moving away from production in the UK – was extraordinarily useful and made our plight a national story.

However with the report finished and delivered to the DCMS, Treasury, and many, many more MPs, we grew frustrated that still the government would not meet with us, respond to the report, or even thank us for figures that were so much more than "numbers on the back of a fag packet". They had promised me due consideration if I made a report and I was not going to let them renege on that! It was time for Plan B.

I blocked out a week, sat down on the internet, and researched every MP, looking for those that would have a vested interest in the wonderful work we produce and the higher up the slippery political pole the better. Did they have children/grandchildren who would watch our shows? Did they have family members in our industry? Or did their job require them to be interested in the business, cultural or educational angle of our campaign? Most importantly, I then cross-referenced the list with constituencies that had animation companies in their local area.

It was via the mechanism of local constituency meetings that I managed to introduce the report to over twenty MPs whom I considered useful allies; these included people with real influence such as Vince Cable, Nick Clegg and David Gauke and, after some protracted negotiations, I procured a meeting with the Chancellor himself!

These meetings proved to be the backbone for the success of the campaign and also gained us access to other MPs. I would like to thank all the animation companies around the country who helped me to gain access to their local MP and who spent the time accompanying me to those meetings.

We knew we were gaining some traction long before the Budget but the weeks before were nervous times while we were waiting. I had a message from Ed Vaizey MP on the morning of the Budget to ask if I was watching – which somewhat gave the game away! – but it made the announcement no less exciting.

Little did I know that more work was to follow in terms of the consultation on the tax credit and the cultural test. But PACT, especially Emily Davidson, stepped up to the plate and we have been able to work with them using many of their resources, to provide the government with everything they need. This support includes Liz Brion (Head of Media Tax) at Grant Thornton, who has supported us free of charge for so long.

With PACT firmly on board we have managed to bring the whole industry together, and while complete agreement within the industry was never going to be possible, as we are not a homogeneous mass, we have presented a united front and have pushed together with one voice, sending the clearest message possible to the Government of what is needed.

We are certain that the tax credit will now go through and be up and running in April, and while we wouldn't like to guess the exact mechanics, it looks like shows that are mostly animated could access around 18% to 20% of their total budgets in the form of a tax rebate; we are all hopeful it offers us enough to put the proud and talented UK animation industry back on the world map. This coupled with a special fund and levy set up to assist with the development of the industry, should see all levels of talent benefit, from university leavers to business owners. Animation in the UK has for too long been held back and disadvantaged, and we had lost so much talent abroad that our industry was facing the precipice. So many of my friends in this industry are no longer trading and doing what they excel at. But now I can see a brighter future. I'm sure we will now see our creative talent flourishing again in the UK with us becoming a nation that is a leader and innovator in animation, and making a real contribution to the creative industries.

The original Saving Animation document

A Little Light Relief ...

An explanation of what's known so far about the new Animation Tax Relief.

Tony Collingwood

The proposed Animation Tax Relief was confirmed by George Osborne in his Autumn Statement.

So what sort of programmes or content will be eligible for this much anticipated 'tax break'? To qualify, at least 51% of the production cost of a programme needs to be spent on animation. This is a valuable concession because many children's programmes are mixed media – they have significant elements of animation without necessarily being entirely animated. Also the programme must be intended for broadcast – but that includes internet platforms.

It is worth noting that projects can only qualify after passing a cultural test. This is based on achieving a number of points from various criteria such as having British or European crews and European subject matter. But animations with "undetermined locations" can also score points in the test, so internationally viable content can still qualify.

The tax relief has been pegged at 25% of the admissible UK core spend. In order to understand how much of a production's actual budget is going to be covered by this tax relief, it is important to dig a little deeper into the detail.

First of all, the amount of UK core spend that is admissible for relief is capped at a maximum of 80%. This is a European rule, which applies in all EU countries, so producers are looking at tax relief on 25% of the 80% core spend.

Illustration by Nick Mackie

opposite page

Also, certain line items are not admissible for tax relief. These have yet to be confirmed by the Government. However we expect that the three main ones will be: the cost of legal services; the cost of borrowing money; and any other grants that go towards your budget – for example an EU Media Grant. So, in real terms, the amount of the full budget eligible for tax relief, on monies spent in the UK, will be approximately 18-20% in cash terms.

We are hoping that the Tax Relief will come into place in the next budget on April 1st. Any money spent on a show before that date will not be eligible. However, if you are already in production before that date, then money spent after that date should be eligible.

Between January and the budget, the plan has to receive EU approval, and work continues on the fine detail - and the explanatory documents from the Government on how to apply. Hopefully, in layman's terms!

Further good news is that the government have offered to match voluntary industry contributions to the Skills Investment Fund managed by Skillset. If the industry put in cash to the Fund, the government will match contributions up to a value of £6 million over two years. We are hoping that those who access the tax break will contribute to the Skillset fund to help train and expand the skills needed for our animation industry.

Children's Media and Ofcom 15
Ofcom

What is Ofcom's statutory role in children's media?
Ofcom has a number of statutory duties in this area, set out below:

Broadcast Programming

Under the Communications Act 2003 ("the Act"), Ofcom has a statutory duty to set standards for broadcast content that will secure the standards' objectives set out in the Act, one of which is "that persons under the age of eighteen are protected".

This duty is reflected in relation to television and radio programmes in Section One of the Ofcom Broadcasting Code ("the Code"). The Code can be viewed at: http://stakeholders.ofcom.org.uk/broadcasting/broadcast-codes/broadcast-code/

The protection of young people under the age of eighteen is one of the key principles upon which the Code is based and is a requirement which we robustly enforce. The protection of children from unsuitable programme content is a responsibility Ofcom must, however, share with carers and parents.

In considering matters of this nature Ofcom must also exercise its duties in a way which is compatible with Article 10 of the European Convention on Human Rights (ECHR). Applied to broadcasting, Article 10 protects the broadcaster's right to transmit material as well as the audience's rights to receive material as long as the broadcaster ensures compliance with the rules of the Code and the requirements of statutory and common law.

The responsibility for Ofcom, therefore, is to balance these broadcaster and audience freedoms against the very important need to give appropriate protection of children, particularly when material is broadcast before the watershed on television, or when children are particularly likely to be listening to radio.

In addition to the rules in Section One that govern the television watershed, there are also more specific rules regarding the protection of children from offensive language, violence, sexual material and the participation of young people in programmes.

Ofcom also has a duty to secure "a wide range of television [...] services which (taken as a whole) are both of high quality and calculated to appeal to a wide range of tastes and interests" provided by "a sufficient plurality of providers of different television [...] services" (section 3(2) of the Act). This applies just as much to children, as to adults. We also have to take account of the desirability of encouraging investment in relevant markets (section 3(4)).

Broadcast Advertising, Sponsorship and Product Placement
In addition to the duties to protect under-eighteens that apply to all broadcast content, there are additional obligations applicable to broadcast advertising, sponsorship and product placement.

Ofcom is required to ensure that the inclusion of advertising which may be misleading, harmful or offensive in television and radio services is prevented. From November 2004, Ofcom delegated day-to-day responsibility for applying the broadcast advertising codes to the ASA. At the same time, responsibility for the TV and Radio Advertising Standards Codes was delegated to the Broadcast Committee of Advertising Practice (BCAP), the industry rule-making body, comprising advertisers, agencies and broadcast media. The UK Code of Broadcast Advertising (BCAP Code)[1] contains, amongst other things, rules that specifically consider the impact of all types of broadcast advertising on children. In addition there are certain products where extra rules are imposed to protect children. Examples include alcohol, food and drink that is high in fat or salt or sugar (HFSS products) and gambling. The restrictions can take two forms:

- Scheduling rules: where and when adverts appear on television
- Content rules: the imagery, wording and tone of the adverts

Ofcom is also required to ensure that the unsuitable sponsorship of programmes included in television and radio services is prevented; and that a variety of safeguards are met with respect to product placement on television, including that product placement is prohibited in television programmes made primarily for children.

Media Literacy

Finally, Section 11 of the Communications Act 2003 places a responsibility on Ofcom regarding the promotion of media literacy. Under Section 14 (6a) of the Act we have a duty to make arrangements for the carrying out of research into the matters mentioned in Section 11 (1) e.g. to "bring about, or to encourage others to bring about, a better public understanding of the nature and characteristics on material published be means of electronic media".

Ofcom fulfils this duty through the annual publication of Media Literacy research into children's/parents' media use and attitudes, as well as those of adults, to enable stakeholders to understand how best to target their media literacy resources. We also conduct additional ad hoc pieces of research in this area as required.

UKCCIS

Whilst not part of its statutory duties, Ofcom sits on the Executive Board of the UK Council for Child Internet Safety (UKCCIS) which brings together over 180 organisations to help keep children and young people safe online. Ofcom is also a member of the UKCCIS Evidence Group, to keep abreast of others' research in this area and ensure that Ofcom's research is shared and used as widely as possible. Ofcom has also participated in a number of other UKCCIS working groups.

What has Ofcom been doing in the children's media arena over the last year?

We have carried out a range of activities in 2012 that have focused on furthering children's interests, either through protection from unsuitable content and other potential risks, or through our research programme which enables ourselves and our stakeholders to understand how the children's media environment is developing.

The Bailey Review

In June 2011, Reg Bailey's review of sexualisation and commercialisation of childhood, *Letting Children be Children,* was published. The report set out a number of recommendations for regulators, broadcasters, industry and a wide range of other stakeholders. The review contained three recommendations which identified specific actions for Ofcom. These covered:

1. The television watershed – enforcement and research;
2. (for all media regulators) The development of a web hub for parents to cover all regulatory complaints about children's exposure to unsuitable or inappropriate material; and
3. Media literacy.

1) Television watershed enforcement and research

In addition to concerns raised by Reg Bailey, Ofcom had already been focusing closely on its enforcement of the watershed. Following some high-profile compliance failures in this area, we conducted meetings with relevant television channels (Channel Television, MTV and WTF) to ensure Ofcom's concerns were clearly understood. These cases involved the broadcast of music videos (Flo Rida and Rihanna's S&M) which breached the Code because they were inappropriately scheduled before the watershed.

We issued new guidance for broadcasters about the acceptability of music videos and material that attracts large family viewing audiences broadcast before and close to the watershed. This detailed guidance drew on key findings from our research on parental attitudes, summarised below. The guidance is available here: http://stakeholders.ofcom.org.uk/binaries/broadcast/guidance/831193/watershed-on-tv.pdf

Outcomes of the new guidance include ensuring industry-wide clarity on compliance requirements around the watershed, more sensitive scheduling, fewer watershed issues/Code breaches, and clear messaging to all stakeholders about how seriously we take the watershed and protection of minors.

Figure 1: Headline findings from Ofcom's pre-watershed research 2011

Of a total of 1,074 parents who were questioned, the majority (58%) were not concerned by the types of things their children have watched on television before 9pm in the last twelve months. 34% of parents were "not at all concerned" and 24% of parents were "not very concerned".

However, 33% of all parents questioned expressed some level of concern about what their children had seen on TV before 9pm in the previous twelve months (findings broadly in line with our media literacy tracker).

Across the group of 1,074 parents, the issues raised spontaneously as being the most important concerns were violence (20%), sexually explicit content (17%) and offensive language (17%). These results were similar to those in our media tracker that focuses on respondents' views about TV in general.

Among all parents questioned, the types of programmes that caused concern were soaps (14%) and film (14%), followed by reality programmes (12%) and music videos (11%).

Source: Research into parents' and teenagers' opinions and concerns on pre-watershed television programming, Ofcom 2011

Following the Bailey review, we commissioned quantitative research among parents/ carers of children from birth to seventeen and separately among teenagers (aged twelve to seventeen). This survey shed further light on the attitudes of parents and teenagers towards content (including music videos) broadcast before the watershed, although it did not indicate as significant a level of concern among parents as was drawn out in the Bailey review research on these same issues.

This parental attitudes survey results can be found at http://stakeholders.ofcom.org.uk/binaries/research/tv-research/ofcom-for-parents/prewatershed-tv-programming.pdf

In addition to our ongoing work on the enforcement of the watershed in television, in December 2011 we published new guidance for radio broadcasters on the use of offensive language. The new guidance was designed to explain the relevant Broadcasting Code rules in more detail and assist radio broadcasters in their compliance with them, with a particular focus on the protection of children in relation to lyrics in music tracks, live music performances, interviews, and studio conversation, and speech and comedy content.

In the first ten months of 2012, Ofcom has launched over 70 investigations of television broadcasters' compliance with our watershed rules. These investigations include cases relating to: offensive language; violence; sexual material; scheduling; transition to more adult material after the watershed; and music videos.

2) Regulators' hub recommendation
The Bailey Review recommended that regulators should work together to create a single website to act as an interface between themselves and parents.

In October 2011 Ofcom joined forces with other UK media regulators to launch http://www.parentport.org.uk, a website to make it easier for parents to complain about material they have seen or heard across the media, communications and retail industries.

The website was jointly developed by the Advertising Standards Authority (ASA), the Authority for Television On Demand (ATVOD), the BBC Trust, the British Board of Film Classification (BBFC), Ofcom, the Press Complaints Commission (PCC) and the Video Standards Council (VSC)/Pan-European Game Information (PEGI).

ParentPort provides straightforward information on what parents can do if they feel they have seen or heard something inappropriate for their children. The site makes the process of making a complaint easier by directing parents to the right regulator for their specific area of concern. The website also provides a "Have Your Say" section, which allows parents to provide informal feedback and comments which regulators will use as an extra gauge of parental views. There is also advice on how to keep children safe online and what parents can do about other products like clothing and the display of magazines in shops.

3) Media literacy education

The Bailey Review also recommended that Ofcom and the BBC "encourage the development of minimum standards guidance for the content of media and commercial literacy education and resources to children".

Ofcom addressed this recommendation through its participation in the UKCCIS project to develop the *Advice on child internet safety 1.0 Universal guidelines for providers*. This initiative not only supplied clear guidance on the media literacy messages that industry should be communicating to children and parents but also provided high quality editorial material for use by any company with an online presence that wishes to use it.

Ofcom's contribution to the project included assessing the evidence base to ensure the selection of the correct key messages for inclusion in the advice; copywriting assistance on editorial content aimed at adults; hosting a UKCCIS event to launch the advice; ensuring the information on the Ofcom website is consistent with the UKCCIS advice; and promoting the advice to stakeholders through our Safer Internet Day communications in early 2012.

Children who participate in programmes

Ofcom's duty to protect the under-eighteens applies not only to children in the viewing or listening audience but also to those children who participate in television and radio programmes. There are two rules in the Broadcasting Code which apply to the participation of those aged under-eighteen in programmes. These rules aim to balance children's right to participate in programmes alongside the requirement that broadcasters take appropriate care of children:

Rule 1.28: Due care must be taken over the physical and emotional welfare and the dignity of people under eighteen who take part or are otherwise involved in programmes. This is irrespective of any consent given by the participant or by a parent, guardian or other person over the age of eighteen in loco parentis.

Rule 1.29: People under eighteen must not be caused unnecessary distress or anxiety by their involvement in programme or by the broadcast of those programmes.

In 2006/7, following an increasing trend in the broadcast of non-fiction programmes involving children and a number of complaints related to children appearing in programmes, Ofcom undertook to review the issues involved in the participation of children in programmes – specifically in non-fiction programmes. Ofcom also considered the need for detailed guidance to accompany Rules 1.28 and 1.29 of the Code. Many other sections of the Code are supported by guidance of this kind.

As part of the process to assess the need for guidance and to gather views on suggestions for its content, we discussed children's participation with broadcasters, programme-makers and PACT, as well as with national and regional children's interest groups, and academic child experts and psychologists.

Ofcom also commissioned independent qualitative research study to explore the views of children and parents on children's participation in non-fiction programmes. You can find it here: http://stakeholders.ofcom.org.uk/binaries/research/tv-research/rpt.pdf

The research showed that both adults and children value and enjoy young people being represented in programmes. However, given that the consequences of participation may vary widely depending on the age, maturity and individual circumstances of the child or young person involved, guidance was seen as a way of helping to safeguard the welfare of under-eighteens during the different stages of their participation in programmes. As a result, Ofcom issued detailed guidance to accompany Rules 1.28 and 1.29. These can be found at pages eleven to fourteen of the following document: http://stakeholders.ofcom.org.uk/binaries/broadcast/guidance/812612/section1.pdf

The Department for Education is currently reviewing The Children's (Performance) Regulations 1968 which govern the licensing by English and Welsh local authorities of children's performances in music, dance, and acting (including on television, in the theatre and on film). Ofcom is working closely with the Department to assist and advise it in this process, along with a number of other relevant stakeholders.

Adult content filtering on BlackBerry devices

In December 2011 it became apparent that it was not possible to block adult web content on BlackBerry devices provided by most of the mobile operators, despite this function generally being available on other mobile handsets.

Ofcom's position on the UKCCIS Board and its links with the mobile sector meant it was well-placed to facilitate discussions between the Mobile Network Operators and the BlackBerry handset manufacturer Research in Motion (RIM), to ensure that consumers on all mobile networks had the option to activate adult content filtering on BlackBerry devices should they wish to do so. This was considered particularly important given the popularity of BlackBerry handsets with children and young people. A filtering solution built by RIM came online in July and was made available to all UK domestic BlackBerry customers by October 2012.

Children's Television

Given our statutory requirements, from time to time we review the provision and consumption of children's programming.

We regularly monitor children's viewing habits through analysis of BARB data, and we ask parents and children via our media literacy tracking surveys (see below) for their opinions about TV content. We also monitor output and spend on the PSB channels and publish this annually as part of our PSB Annual Report. This report also contains information on parents' views about whether PSB broadcasters deliver 'a wide range of high quality, UK-made programmes for children'.[2]

Figure 2: Viewing to children's and adult airtime, 2007 and 2011 Media literacy research

WEEKLY VIEWING (%)	2011	2007	2011	2007	2011	2007
	CHILDREN 4-15	CHILDREN 4-15	CHILDREN 4-9	CHILDREN 4-9	CHILDREN 10-15	CHILDREN 10-15
% TOTAL TIME SPENT IN ADULT AIRTIME	66	68	53	56	80	80
% TOTAL TIME SPEND IN CHILDREN'S AIRTIME	33	32	47	41	20	20

Despite the many competing attractions, recent research from BARB shows that television continues to be very important to children. In 2011, they watched a total of 17.34 hours a week, 1.8 hours more than in 2005.

Children watch a lot of programming in adult air time, as Figure 2 shows. This has changed relatively little in the last five years. Overall, 66% of children's viewing is to adult TV, and 33% to children's television. As children get older, their viewing habits change. While 47% of the viewing of children aged four to nine is to children's programming, older children (ten to fifteen) watch comparatively little children's television – 80% of their viewing is to adult programming.

Looking at post-watershed viewing, specifically 9pm to midnight, the proportion of children watching television during this time has remained steady since 2010 at 14%. In 2007 the figure was 12%. Among four to nine year olds the figure rose from 8% in 2007 to 9% in 2011. Among the ten to fifteen year old age group it was 15% in 2007, increasing to 18% in 2010 and returning to 15% in 2011.

There is a wide range of adult programming, particularly in family viewing time, that is easily accessible to older children, such as drama (e.g. *Dr Who, Hollyoaks, Merlin*), comedy (e.g. *Walk on the Wild Side, Harry Hill's TV Burp*), animation (e.g. *The Simpsons*), factual entertainment (e.g. *Brainiac, Traffic Cops, Mythbusters, Top Gear*), entertainment (e.g. *Total Wipeout*), popular music (e.g. *UKHot40: The Top 20*), and history (e.g. *Wartime Farm*).

Media use and attitudes report

Figure 3: Media activity children aged 5-15 would miss the most: 2007, 2008, 2009, 2010, 2011 and 2012

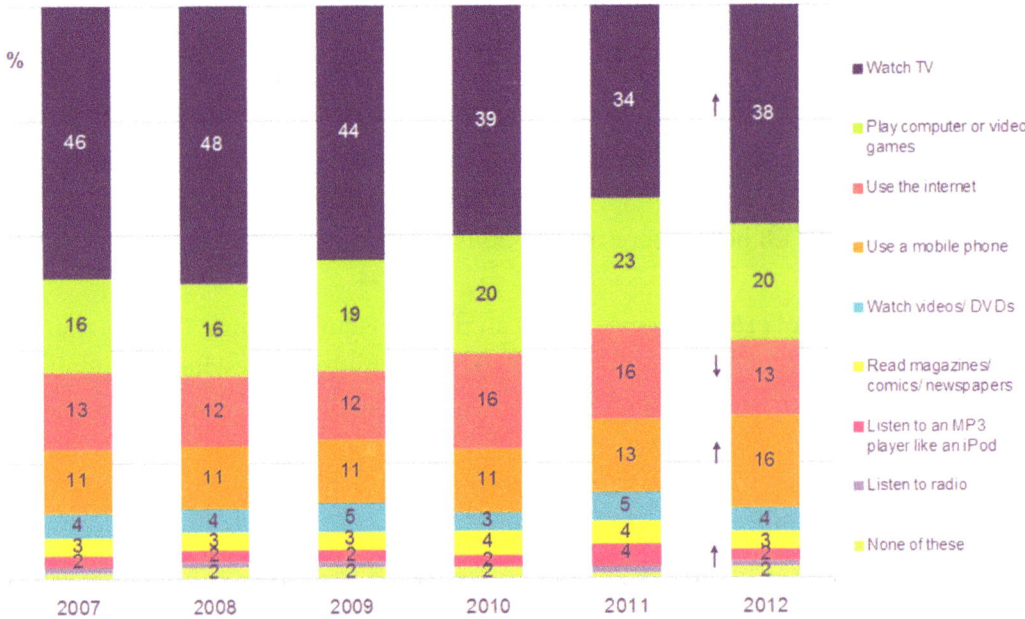

QC55 – WHICH ONE OF THE THINGS YOU DO ALMOST EVERY DAY, WOULD YOU MISS DOING THE MOST IF IT GOT TAKEN AWAY? (PROMPTED RESPONSES, SINGLE CODED)
BASE: CHILDREN AGED 5-15 (3696 AGED 5-15 IN 2007, 2066 AGED 5-15 IN 2008, 2131 AGED 5-15 IN 2009, 2071 AGED 5-15 IN 2010, 1717 AGED 5-15 IN 2011, 1717 AGED 5-15 IN 2012). SIGNIFICANCE TESTING SHOWS ANY DIFFERENCE BETWEEN 2011 AND 2012
SOURCE: OFCOM RESEARCH, FIELDWORK CARRIED OUT BY SAVILLE ROSSITER-BASE IN MARCH 2012

Ofcom's *Children and Parents: Media Use and Attitudes* report was published in October 2012.[3]

Ofcom's research is a key source of trend data about children's internet habits and opinions, and about parents' strategies to protect their children online. It provides detailed evidence of media use, attitudes and understanding among children and young people aged five to fifteen. For the first time in 2012 it also provides information about the access to, and use of, media among children aged three to four.

In 2012, 1717 parents and children aged five to fifteen were interviewed, and 190 parents of children aged three to four. Questions covered access and use of TV, radio, the internet, mobile phones and games, and opinions and behaviour relating to online safety and privacy habits, critical understanding and knowledge.

The surveys have been running since 2005 and therefore many trends over time can be plotted, as illustrated in Figure 3, which sets out how the media that children say they would miss the most has changed over time.

Parental controls

In addition to our regular monitoring of parental controls in our quantitative survey, this year we decided to look in more depth at the reasons that lay behind the use or non-use of technical parental controls which enable parents to block access to content that they may consider to be inappropriate for their children. We commissioned qualitative research,[4] and asked 85 parents for their views.

The aims of the research were to provide evidence of parents' attitudes to, and experience of, parental controls for internet enabled devices; and to understand how parental controls fit within the wider repertoire of parents' mediation of their child's internet/media use. The research began by exploring overall approaches to parenting. This provided a broader contextual understanding of how parenting approaches influence the response both to parental controls specifically and internet mediation more widely.

Our survey data and the qualitative research formed the basis of Ofcom's response to the Government's consultation on parental controls in the autumn of 2012.

Figure 4: Summary of parental controls in place, by platform: 2012

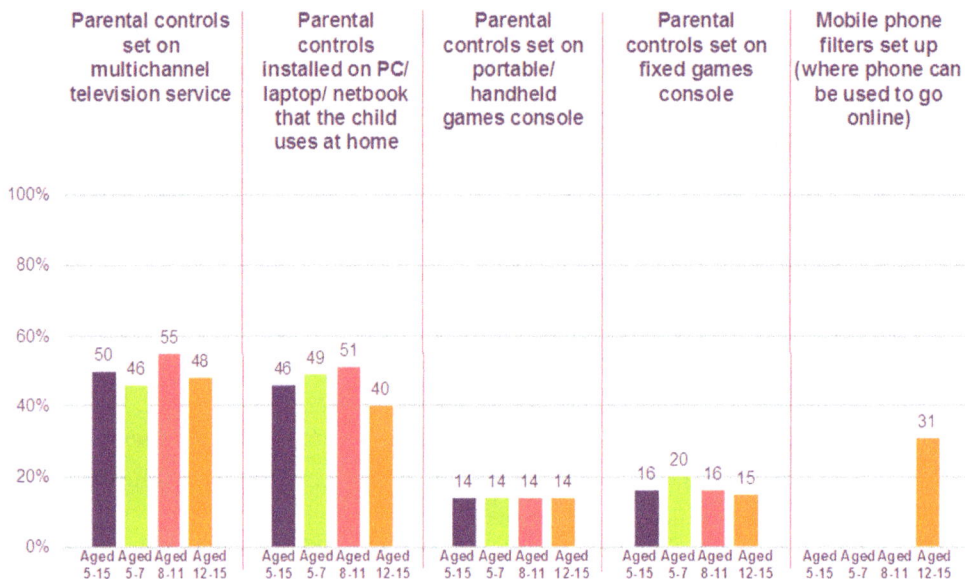

QP13/ QP32/ QP77/ QP78/ QP70 – Does your television service have any parental controls set to stop certain programmes, films or channels being viewed on your TV, until a PIN or password is entered?/ Just to check do you have any of these types of 'parental controls' loaded or put into place and working on the PC/laptop/netbook that your child uses at home to prevent them viewing certain types of website?/ Are there any parental controls set on the handheld games console?/ Are there any parental controls set on the games console that is connected to a TV?/ Is access to the internet on your child's phone limited to exclude websites that are aimed at people aged 18 and over?

Base: Parents of children aged 5-15 who watch multichannel TV at home/ Parents whose child aged 5-15 uses a PC/laptop or netbook to go online at home/ Parents of children aged 5-15 with a portable games console/ Parents of children aged 5-15 with a fixed games console/ Parents of 12-15s with a mobile phone that can be used to go online – Significance testing shows any change between 2011 and 2012

Source: Ofcom research, fieldwork carried out by Saville Rossiter-Base in March 2012

Looking ahead: Ofcom's focus in 2013

Parental Controls

The role of parental controls in helping to keep children safe online will remain the subject of considerable debate amongst policy makers in the UK and Europe in 2013. Parental controls are an important tool for parents across a range of media and communications services and Ofcom will continue to contribute to the discussion through its media literacy research and in its role as an Executive Board member of UKCCIS.

Research projects

We will continue our media use and attitudes work, with fieldwork in the spring of 2013 and reporting in the autumn, with a continued examination of younger children aged three to four. We will consider the need to carry out further research as needed.

Standards

We will continue to monitor closely broadcasters' compliance with the rules in Section One of the Code on the protection of children, and will take robust regulatory action where necessary.

Watershed

We will continue to conduct research on parents' views on the watershed on an annual basis. We are currently assessing the latest 2012 responses.

ParentPort

The ParentPort regulators are currently working on new ways to raise parents' awareness of ParentPort and develop the site.

Further information on Ofcom's approach to protection of children

Please find out more about our work in this area in the new dedicated consumers. ofcom.org.uk/parents/ of our website. Our research is available at ofcom.org.uk/ medialiteracyresearch.

---------- NOTES --------------------

1. The BCAP Code can be found at http://www.cap.org.uk/Advertising-Codes/Broadcast-HTML.aspx

2. http://stakeholders.ofcom.org.uk/broadcasting/reviews-investigations/ublic-service-broadcasting/annrep/psb12/

3. http://stakeholders.ofcom.org.uk/binaries/research/media-literacy/oct2012/main.pdf

4. http://stakeholders.ofcom.org.uk/binaries/research/media-literacy/oct2012/Annex_1.pdf

Speaking Out 16
Research, Public Debate and Policy
David Buckingham

In October 2012, the *Guardian* newspaper ran a front page story headlined "Ban under-threes from watching television, says study".[1] Based on a review of research published in the *Archives of Disease in Childhood* (a BMJ journal), it reported that doctors at the Royal College of Paediatrics and Child Health were "increasingly concerned" about the impact on television viewing on children's brain development. The author of the review was calling for a complete ban on "screen time" for under-threes, rising gradually to a limit of two hours for those aged sixteen and over – recommendations that go further than those apparently made in other countries, by bodies such as the American Academy of Paediatrics. The *Guardian* story was subsequently picked up by the BBC and a range of other media outlets; and I myself was interviewed for Sky News.

The author of the original review was not, in fact, an academic or a paediatrician but a well-known anti-television campaigner, Aric Sigman – the author of popular books such as *The Spoilt Generation* and *Remotely Controlled: How Television is Damaging Our Lives*. Sigman frequently claims that the only authorities who should be consulted on the question of children and television are doctors, although he himself is not a doctor: he has a PhD in psychology, although he is not a practising psychologist either. Nor indeed is he a researcher: he has never conducted his own research about children and television, or indeed any other media. His article for the *Archives of Disease in Childhood* consists of an extremely partial review of the available research, hardly any of which relates specifically to children under the age of three. It concentrates exclusively on psychological 'effects' research, and fails to mention (let alone address) the many theoretical and methodological challenges that have been made to these kinds of studies – although it does insinuate those who disagree with this view are merely in the pay of the television industry. Its concluding recommendations are, to say the least, unwarranted by the evidence that is reviewed.

This story is not untypical, but it raises some interesting questions about the nature of public debate about children and media. Why did such an apparently reputable academic journal – and its peer reviewers – accept such a partial and inadequate review by an author who is known, not as a medical practitioner or a researcher, but as a campaigner? Why did a serious newspaper like the *Guardian* give the story front-page coverage, and pay so little attention to those who challenged his views? On what basis should institutions like the Royal College of Paediatrics and Child Health issue recommendations to parents on such matters? And what can researchers who actually work in this area do to present a better informed perspective, and generate a more balanced and sensible public debate?

Like many academic researchers who work in this field, I receive frequent requests to respond to media enquiries. In the past few months, I have had numerous requests of this kind. A news report about two fourteen year olds who made their own pornographic video led to an invitation from a mass-circulation daily newspaper to write an opinion piece about "the sexualisation of childhood". The murder of twelve people at the screening of the latest *Batman* movie in Aurora, Colorado, prompted a request from a radio news channel for my views on the effects of media violence. Most recently, I was asked for my opinions about the impact of mobile phone 'apps': are they (and I quote) making us "lazy and solipsistic" or do they "open new avenues of life" and promote "even faster brain processing"? Alongside this have been discussions with a documentary producer about the contribution of media and consumer culture to the phenomenon of 'nature deficit disorder' among children; a query about the effects of reading e-books on children's imagination and attention span; and a request for a radio interview about whether there should be age-based ratings for children's books like those for apparently more 'harmful' media such as film and video.

My response to these kinds of queries is, I confess, often ambivalent and conflicted. In fact, I frequently ignore or decline them – and yet I often feel guilty and even ashamed about doing so. Of course, some of these questions are ones that I am ill-equipped to answer, and on which little useful evidence is available – although that does not always appear to be a significant constraint for some of those who *do* choose to respond to them.

However, my avoidance of such queries primarily reflects my impatience with the terms in which the public debate about children and the media is typically defined. This is largely an either/or debate, about whether the media are 'good' or 'bad' for children. It is a debate that (as with some of my examples above) is often prompted by rare and spectacular events – yet these events are nevertheless frequently seen to be typical, or to tell us something much more broadly about the direction in which our society is heading. And it often leads on to a discussion about whether we should restrict or control children's access to media, or indeed the media themselves. Framing the debate in these terms focuses attention on a narrow range of phenomena, and seriously restricts what can possibly be said about them. Yet the ways in which this agenda is set in the wider public domain inevitably exert a significant influence on the formation of policy and, by extension, on the funding of further research.

Academics in the UK – and elsewhere – are increasingly urged to consider the question of *impact*. In applying for government research grants and in competing for funding under the "Research Excellence Framework" (REF) we are now required to identify 'pathways to impact' and to produce 'impact narratives' showing how our work has influenced policy and practice beyond the academy. We might question whether such an apparently aggressive term is well chosen: most of us would probably prefer the increasingly popular, and more dialogical, notion of 'public engagement'. However, most academics are surely concerned that their work will make a difference to the wider world: the 'impact agenda' may provide a useful means of recognising and rewarding this.

Nevertheless, achieving, demonstrating and measuring impact is bound to be a complex matter. One significant difficulty here is that we have only limited opportunities, and limited power, to determine how our work will be represented in the public domain. As such, the relationships between research, media coverage, public debate and policy-making, which are the focus of this article, are almost bound to prove difficult and troubling.

Three exhibits

The following three brief examples, taken from recent UK debates about children, young people and media, illustrate some of the ways in which academics *are* able to contribute to these discussions. They also point to some of the formidable difficulties we face in generating a more constructive public debate.

Susan Greenfield is Professor of Synaptic Pharmacology at Oxford University, and a former director of the Royal Institution. She is also a Baroness: an appointed member of the House of Lords. Over the past few years, Professor Greenfield has made a number of high-profile public statements about the effects of the internet and other digital media on children's brain development. The targets of her concern are fairly broad-ranging, as a sample of her many recent headlines suggests:

> Facebook addicts can't relate, says scientist Susan Greenfield
>
> Texting 'could increase attention deficit disorders' says Baroness Greenfield
>
> Social websites harm children's brains: Chilling warning to parents from top neuroscientist
>
> Susan Greenfield: Computers may be altering our brains [2]

Greenfield's claims are partly based on neuroscientific theories about the plasticity of the developing human brain; although she also claims that electronic media have caused a wider loss of 'empathy' within contemporary society, manifested in the apparent rise in violence, addiction, and so on. In 2011, controversy arose when Professor Greenfield claimed that the internet was responsible for the rise in childhood autism – a claim that clearly does not stand up to even the briefest critical interrogation. Greenfield's claims were publicly challenged by one of her academic colleagues, Professor Dorothy Bishop, an expert on autism, and by autism campaigners. In this case, as in others, Greenfield agreed (when pressed) that the evidence was limited; although she also asserted that the issue was so urgent that the lack of definitive evidence did not matter, and that action should be taken right away.[3]

David Starkey is a former Professor of History at the London School of Economics, and the author of numerous apparently definitive texts on British constitutional history. He is also a frequent media commentator. In August 2011, he appeared on the BBC's flagship news magazine programme, *Newsnight,* in a discussion of the rioting that had erupted in many UK cities earlier that week. Starkey argued that the riots were a result of the influence of black culture on white working-class young people, especially through media such as rap music:

> What's happened is that a substantial section of the chavs … have
> become black. The whites have become black. A particular sort of violent,
> destructive, nihilistic, gangster culture has become the fashion … And this is
> why so many of us have this sense of [England as] literally a foreign country
> …[4]

When questioned, Starkey was unable to name any examples of rap music, but he was by no means alone in pointing to the media as a cause of the riots. Commentary in the wake of these events frequently laid the blame on media as diverse as computer games, rap music, reality television, social networking sites and the advertising of designer clothing. Starkey is well known as a controversialist, but he is also an historian. In inviting him to contribute, the producers of *Newsnight* might perhaps have expected him to offer a considered historical perspective. Yet this was not what he provided; and his contribution raises significant questions about the uses and abuses of academic authority.

Dr. Linda Papadopoulos is a child psychologist who was commissioned by the UK government to produce an official report on the "sexualisation of young people", which was published in 2010. The report arose in the context of a Home Office review of domestic violence against women, instigated by the then Labour Home Secretary Jacqui Smith; although Conservative politicians, including Prime Minister David Cameron, have also complained about the 'creepy sexualisation' of girls in music videos, fashion advertising, teenage magazines and other media. The incoming Conservative government subsequently commissioned a further report on this issue from Mr. Reg Bailey, the chief executive of the Mothers' Union (a Christian charity). Bailey's report, symptomatically entitled *Letting Children Be Children*, recommended a range of restrictions on media and marketing that are currently being followed through.

Dr. Papadopoulos is a practising clinical psychologist who is also employed at the University of North London. Her own research has been primarily in the field of dermatology. However, she is also a glamorous celebrity: she has appeared as the resident psychologist on *Big Brother*, and is regularly used as an 'expert' on breakfast television. She has also featured on programmes such as *Celebrity Mastermind* and *Celebrity Fit Club*. 'Dr. Linda' (as she prefers to be known in these contexts) also runs a private beauty consultancy for women, which markets its own range of beauty products.

Papadopoulos's report is dominated by psychological theories of media effects: there is no discussion of research using sociological or Cultural Studies perspectives, or of the many criticisms of media effects research.[5] Her statements to journalists typically align this account with a pathological view of contemporary young women:

> It is a drip, drip effect. Look at porn stars, and look how an average girl
> now looks. It's seeped into every day: fake breasts, fuck-me shoes ... We are
> hypersexualising girls, telling them that their desirability relies on being
> desired. They want to please at any cost.[6]

Predictably, the Papadopoulos report and the ensuing debate received wide media coverage, not least because it provided a pretext for the media to feature examples of the offending material: perhaps the most notable was the website of the *Daily Mail* – a newspaper well known for its moral campaigning – which featured several raunchy images of the star Rihanna while simultaneously calling on the media regulator Ofcom to ban them.

Conditions of authority

As these examples suggest, debates about young people and the media are a constant concern for the media themselves. Behind the three I have discussed, stand a legion of commentators, pundits and campaigners willing to recite their views about the harmful effects of the media, seemingly at any passing invitation. Aside from the lunatic fringe represented by Aric Sigman and members of the White Dot Society, they would include the outgoing Archbishop of Canterbury, Rowan Williams, whose views on the 'Disneyfication' of modern childhood have been widely cited; and the parenting 'expert' Sue Palmer, whose bestseller *Toxic Childhood: How the Modern World is Damaging our Children and What We Can Do About It* (2006) has set much of the agenda for contemporary discussion.

However, my three 'exhibits' are all academics. Of course, they might be disparaged as media celebrities: despite their readiness to blame the media, they are all exceptionally 'media-friendly'. Nevertheless, the first two at least are undoubtedly distinguished in their respective fields. They carry a degree of academic authority and gravitas, which is strongly endorsed by official bodies (the Royal Institution, the BBC, the government). They purport to present scientific evidence, and to embody the wisdom of disciplined scholarship. Paradoxically, the fact that none of them has any experience whatsoever in media research may be seen as an advantage: they all come from academic disciplines that are generally seen as more serious and legitimate than Media Studies – a field whose claims to authority are still widely vilified in the mainstream media.

Media researchers are, of course, somewhat inured to the phenomenon of 'blaming the media'. In different ways, my three exhibits all reflect the familiar characteristics of this approach: the media are regarded as a primary, if not exclusive, cause of very broad (and frequently ill-defined) social phenomena; they are seen to operate according to a simple cause-and-effect logic, in which audiences are merely passive victims of media manipulation; and these effects are routinely displaced onto *other* people (especially young people) who are deemed to be incompetent or dysfunctional consumers.

What is particularly notable is how the concept of *childhood* is invoked in these debates. For campaigners, childhood provides a valuable 'hot button' - a convenient symbol that helps to focus much broader fears and aspirations about social change. Framing the issue in generational terms typically invokes generalisations about childhood: the child is defined in sentimental terms, either as helpless and vulnerable or as exotic and spontaneously competent. Framing the relationship in terms of *effects* necessarily implies a concept of causality, in which the media are seen as an external force, impacting upon children's lives from outside. The issue of children's relationships with media is thus typically framed in either/or terms, in which the media are either 'good' or 'bad' for them – an approach which precludes the asking of other questions, not least about how children themselves understand these issues.

These particular ways of framing the topic lead inexorably to proposals at the level of public policy that verge on the absurd, as though we could isolate the bad elements and remove them, leaving only the good. In the wake of the UK riots, for example, it was seriously suggested that the police should 'turn off the internet' in order to prevent young people collecting on the streets; while the debate about sexualisation has led to the proposal for 100-metre exclusion zones around schools, from which 'sexualised' imagery would be banned.

Media researchers know that generations of scholars have shown the role of the media in society to be significantly more diverse and complex than this. Yet in the public debate, the *persistence* of media-blaming and of simplistic assertions about media effects is undeniable. However much we may wearily insist that 'it's much more complicated than that', the debate continues to be framed in terms of assertions that, on the contrary, it is actually very simple indeed.

Terms of engagement

In this situation, it is often hard to imagine how academic research might make a more effective contribution to public knowledge. Yet this is surely a vital question – not least because the public debate itself plays a significant role in setting the agenda for policy and (whether we like it or not) for academic work itself. In the field of science communication, there has been a significant shift in recent years from the notion of 'public understanding of science' to that of 'public engagement with science': this new perspective moves beyond the deficit model of a passive, ignorant public that is in need of being informed by scientific experts, towards a greater emphasis on dialogue. Yet when it comes to social science, the relations between public knowledge, evidence and policy are likely to be more complex and contested. Compared with natural scientists, the authority of social scientific 'experts' is inevitably more open to question, both within and beyond their own disciplines. Furthermore, the topics on which social scientists work tend to be much closer to people's everyday experience. Arguably, we are not all equally entitled to express an opinion about quantum mechanics or global warming, or at least judged to be equally credible if we attempt to do so; whereas it would seem that anybody – from the Archbishop of Canterbury to your local taxi-driver – is equally entitled to hold a view about whether television or computer games are good or bad for children.

This can result in a widespread suspicion amongst academics about the value of media engagement. Such engagement is often perceived to entail a form of 'popularisation' or even 'vulgarisation'; and those colleagues who do pursue it are sometimes condemned as 'media whores'. This condemnation also extends to academics who are busily using social media: academic twittering and social networking are often ridiculed as merely forms of self-promotion. These complaints are not without justification in some cases: academic self-publicists risk fatally undermining their own legitimacy, to the point where even mainstream media may come to see them as unworthy of being taken seriously.

Of course, it might seem quite utopian to expect that the media might ever function as a rational 'public sphere', or as a realm of pure communication in which scientific evidence could be transparently represented. Perhaps media academics should know better than to expect that nuanced, qualified accounts of the complex, multi-factorial nature of media influence are somehow going to make the headlines. Yet however much we may distrust simplistic media coverage, our managers and employers may feel that there is rarely such a thing as bad publicity. There are certainly instances where the attempts of university press offices to publicise particular instances of research have resulted in inaccurate forms of media 'spin', in which academics themselves have occasionally been complicit.[7]

Finally, there is the question of how such debates feed into policy. The notion of 'evidence-based policy' assumes that evidence is an unproblematic phenomenon, and that it can simply be accumulated, like picking apples from a tree; it belies the fact that policy-making has its own dynamics, which are subject to much wider forces. The debate around the 'sexualisation of childhood' (discussed above) provides many instances of this, as did my own experience of leading a parallel UK government review - *The impact of the commercial world on children's wellbeing*.[8] Far from pursuing 'evidence-based policy', my abiding impression was that politicians were themselves highly subject to the vicissitudes of media coverage: rather than setting the terms of debate, they were often improvising in response to emerging expressions of 'public opinion' as articulated by the right-wing press – a situation that is paradoxical in light of the continuing decline in newspaper circulation.

Conclusion

I have written this article partly as a provocation to further debate among the research community in particular; although it is probably clear that I am having some kind of debate with myself. As researchers, I feel we should be doing a better job in communicating our research to the wider public. Yet I am weary of working in a situation where the terms of debate are predefined in ways that are exasperatingly narrow, and where there are such powerful constraints on what can possibly be said. In an age of 'social media', we might expect this to be getting easier, as we are able to exercise greater control over the channels and means of communication that we use – although, as we become merely another voice amid the babble of online discussion, it seems much more likely that academic authority and credibility will be further undermined. A body such as the Children's Media Foundation - which brings together researchers, media producers, parents, policy makers and other interested parties - might be uniquely placed to make a difference to this situation: I hope that it will.

---------- Notes --------------------

1. See http://www.guardian.co.uk/society/2012/oct/09/ban-under-threes-watching-television. Sigman's review was published as 'Time for a view on screen time', *Archives of Disease in Childhood*, 8th October 2012, archdischild-2012-302196.

2. These headlines are from: *Sydney Morning Herald*, June 9th 2010; *Daily Telegraph* 12th August 2009; *Daily Mail* 24th February 2009; *Independent* 12th August 2011.

3. For further details on this debate, see: http://www.guardian.co.uk/society/2011/aug/06/research-autism-internet-susan-greenfield.

4. Starkey's contribution was available on YouTube:
http://www.youtube.com/watch?v=gU5TcTSa9kk.

5. The report is available online at: http://webarchive.nationalarchives.gov.uk/+/homeoffice.gov.uk/about-us/news/sexualisation-young-people.html. Papadopoulos's own site is www.drlinda.com.

6. This quotation comes from the *Guardian*, 25th February 2011.

7. In late 2011 I appeared, alongside Professor Susan Greenfield, in an edition of BBC Radio 4's *The Media Show*, which discussed some interesting instances of this: this programme (tx. 28th December 2011) is still available at www.bbc.co.uk/programmes/b018gqzy.

8. The report is online at:
 https://www.education.gov.uk/publications/standard/publicationDetail/Page1/DCSF-00669-2009

RESEARCH HIGHLIGHTS

REPLAY REPEAT CLUE MYSTERY WORD SECRET CODE LETTER SAY IT SPELL

ON

B C D E F G H I J
L M N O P Q R S T
V W X Y Z

MODULE SELECT ERASE ENTER

eak & Spell

Whatever people say I am, that's what I'm not … (the extended mix)

17

Becky Parry

In the UK, children are all too often collectively and problematically described: they are seen as constantly in danger whilst also posing a threat; the exams they take are too easy and yet they take more national exams in their life course than any other nation. Headlines could lead us to conclude that there is a constant crisis in relation to childhood. Children's media is also often implicated in these debates and it will be interesting to see if, in the next few months, it is guns or games with guns that are the subject of new legislation in the US. It is important that we care about what children watch and play and that the media industry continue to create imaginative and stimulating media for them. However, our concern should be proportional, less keen to attribute blame, and informed by the diverse experiences of children.

Media educators and those making media for children are in a unique position to share ideas about contemporary childhood and to question the standard tropes that children are multi-tasking, tech-savvy, digital natives who are simultaneously vulnerable to and obsessed by celebrity and material culture. I hope this publication stimulates an exchange about children, media research and education, thereby also usefully informing public debate. Flying in the face of my grandmother's idiom that 'names will never hurt', what we call children, how we care, parent, educate and entertain them, *does* matter and so, at least for now, we should care about whatever 'people' say about them.

Not only children, but also children's media, are frequently the butt of criticism, so teaching children about media is derided, and indeed, in some circles, Media Studies has become a byword for all that is wrong about the contemporary education system. Few subject areas are as vilified or as wilfully misunderstood, and the subject is increasingly marginalised. Once more, it is essential to challenge 'whatever people say' – and, despite the rapid growth and innovation in digital industries, people like the Secretary of State for Education (and the odd journalist) do increasingly say that media education is a 'soft' option.

In the context of the primary classroom, with some noticeable exceptions, media education remains peripheral and children's participation in media cultures is often a cause for concern for educators (Lambirth, 2004). To some, it is alarming to consider that television programmes, popular music or console games might infiltrate classrooms in place of 'higher value' texts, and media is certainly conspicuous by its absence in the new draft of the National Curriculum for Primary English. A traditional defence of the inclusion of popular culture has been that, by doing so, we counter media saturation and arm children against influence. These arguments are well rehearsed but, for me, that is something else that media education is not.

Children engage with a rich "narrative web" of popular culture texts and artefacts through which they explore identity and develop literacy (Marsh, 2005). By the time children go to school they have already built up a repertoire of "symbolic resources" they use to enable talk and play (Buckingham and Sefton-Green, 1994; Pahl, 2006). Children's media are complex, sophisticated and pleasurable narratives, and children read them actively, collectively and culturally. If we do not pay attention to how they read them and how they might also proceed to make them, we lose the opportunity for them to engage with their own lived experience of literacy. Teachers too, live media-rich lives and have developed tastes and preferences which contribute to their identities and orientation to literacy (Buckingham et al., 2010). At school, children are taught to read, write, speak and listen through extensive use of narrative texts. However, for many children there is a disconnect between their home and school experiences of narrative (Parry, 2010). Contemporary policy, a restrictive literacy curriculum and a prescriptive pedagogy, all result in many of the shared experiences of children and teachers being left outside the classroom door. For some children then, everything they know about stories, based on popular culture texts, is not valued and is therefore not an asset to them. Given the centrality of narrative to literacy teaching, these children are likely to fail, and are being failed by current practices relating to the teaching of literacy which rule out contemporary culture and place too much emphasis on decontextualised writing skills. This is a missed opportunity and leaves children and young people feeling alienated from the curriculum, school and learning.

Media education as a form of protectionism obscures the potential to acknowledge what Williams (1989) described as the distinct importance of narrative to our culture. The affective, social, and cultural relationships children develop with media need to be valued as part of their experience of narrative. There is also an urgent need to enable children to draw on their experiences of media in order to make explicit their understandings of the affordances of different multimodal forms. Stories are no longer only in print form and children need to be taught to read and infer meaning in all forms, including moving image. We still only have emerging models of learning progression for literacy (a perception of literacy which incorporates all the types of texts children engage with) and there remains a pressing need for contemporary research in this area. The negative perceptions of children's media texts and media education obscures these questions and constrains important areas of research. There is a growing body of work however, within the paradigm of New Literacies, which explores the relationship between children's participation in contemporary media, and their emerging literacy and identity practices both at home and at school. This work needs further dissemination. However, there remains an urgent need to examine children and young people's contemporary literacies as they play out in schools.

David Buckingham's ESRC funded project, 'Developing Media Literacy: Towards a Model of Learning Progression'[1] has begun to demonstrate that it is not enough to value children's experiences of media. Nor is it enough to develop media literacy in order to enhance school-based literacies. Children as young as six can understand and begin to apply new sets of questions to texts and experiences that are clearly advancing their understandings of their own lived culture. Last year, I observed a Year Three classroom in Croydon where children conducted, collated and analysed audience research, leading them to recognise that different audiences might interpret or make sense and meaning from texts in different ways. I also observed a Year Five class in Cambridge make radio news broadcasts, learning not only about the process of production but also about regulation, funding and news values. More broadly, both groups of children were learning that texts are constructed: they represent the world in particular ways and so audiences, including themselves, respond to them actively, socially and culturally. Interestingly, these children voiced interest in the Leveson enquiry; the role of a public service broadcaster; why news is obsessed by celebrity; and whether it is important to tell the truth. I would suggest that this is evidence of productive and challenging learning.

The children in these projects were also able to articulate understandings of abstract concepts such as modality, empathy, point of view, intertextuality and irony: concepts more often left to much older students to grapple with. To return to my premise, people say that media education is a 'soft option', when in reality, a 'soft option' is clearly what it is not!

The negative perceptions of media education undermine the very useful research which is undertaken in this area and obscures important, specific and distinct questions. It is very easy to get headlines by declaring childhood is toxic (as every generation has in one form or another) but to undertake research with children about their engagement with media is a much less headline grabbing project. In the last few months I have been privileged to work with the digital arts organization Lovebytes and Year Six children at a primary school in Hillsborough, Sheffield. Funded by First Light and in collaboration with the Institute of Education, I have been researching children's contemporary film production practices at home and school. The planning and development for the project was underpinned by this proposition by Gunther Kress (1995:75):

> The means for making representations which we provide for children and for adults, are the means which enable them to be fully human and fully social.

That is to say, that the visual and moving image media are at least as significant to children, as forms of expression or means of storytelling, as the written word. Historically, comparatively few children make films either at home or at school and despite considerable technological innovation, it remains a marginal activity only accessed by the few. 'The few' tend to have access not only to technology and software but perhaps more importantly, to family expertise, support and timely interventions and, furthermore, an audience. Willett (2009) describes Jacob, twelve, who produced a complex and captivating skateboard film which was shared online. Jacob had strong family support for his activity and so had access to the participatory media culture which Jenkins (2009) describes. By contrast, in my own doctoral research (Parry, 2010), I shared the experience of Connor, who had used his gran's phone to create a film because he was bored. He described the making process here:

> I've made that. It's not exactly a film. I've made up a voice. I've got a couple of teddies. I got her phone and I put it on video and what I did so it didn't see my hand. I kept pressing the pause button and then I moved it into a different place and pressed play [means record] and then spoke a bit and then moved it again.

Connor describes using a stop motion animation technique, voice over and editing in camera, and displays considerable intrinsic motivation. Being a storyteller was a strong aspect of Connor's identity but his stories were moving image stories and at home and at school he did not receive adult support to pursue his interest, neither did his work (in this case) reach an audience. Thus, Connor, like many other children for whom films are rich narrative sources, was at a disadvantage if he did not have opportunities to make films.

The Sheffield project was, therefore, designed to be able to inform future practice in terms of building bridges between young people's informal home-based film production practices, and film production activity they might encounter in more formal spaces such as schools, after school clubs or special projects. The company Lovebytes was the long-standing project partner who developed, planned and delivered the film production activity, following extensive meetings with myself as the researcher for the Sheffield project. Our discussions focused on our previous experiences of the creative process in film production projects with children and we were very keen to avoid some pitfalls we felt we had previously observed. For example, we felt it was critical that the children felt this was an exploratory and experimental project which allowed them to try and retry different approaches to film production. We felt that we wanted to enable the children to identify stories they were interested in telling, and questions they wanted to ask about how film is made, rather sticking to ideas we had tentatively suggested in our funding application process.

Having also observed many film production processes in which the children were allowed only token involvement, we wanted to ensure they had a high degree of autonomy and involvement in every aspect of production. As a consequence we took an experimental approach to the role of the adult and to the planning of provocations or creative 'missions' which the children undertook, in order to see which were most effective in scaffolding understanding and extending learning. Furthermore, we wanted to ensure that every activity we attempted could be tried at home independently, should the children be keen to have a go. We agreed that connecting the activities with children's rich repertoires of moving image as a medium that they engage with through talk, play and text production, would be an important aspect of our approach. In the course of the project we found that it was important to draw on the school space in which we were working as a rich resource for exploring ideas too.

An initial questionnaire played an important role in gaining data about the children's previous experiences of home and school film production, and this data did not fit entirely with what we may have expected. The Sheffield data did not reveal that the Year Six children were engaged in innovative or online film production practices. Although some of the children did indicate that they made films at home many of these were unedited and, on the whole, not shared online. We were keen to use this project as an opportunity to explore why this was the case. This was a question that was asked throughout the film production process and became part of what could be described as an ongoing research conversation, developing our understanding of the support children might need to undertake film production at home.

At the outset of each project we asked each group about what ideas they had which could be turned into films, and what questions they had about film production. Lovebytes used these ideas as a basis for planning ideas for activities. For example, one group of children were very keen to explore film in terms of perception, that is to say, in film, how do we make people fly, turn invisible, disappear, look like ghosts? We used these ideas to develop an activity which would enable them to experiment with how this was done.

We were also keen to extend the children's understanding and vocabulary in relation to film language. Some of the modes of film are less explicitly understood than others, so, for example, children often identify costume as a key meaning-making device, but not shot composition or temporal organisation (Parry, 2010). We wanted to gain understanding of effective and productive ways of teaching film language. We therefore identified some key concepts such as time (continuity and flashback), fly-on-the-wall (documenting the real), close-up, point of view, movement and animation and explored many ideas for teaching these concepts. We did not stick rigidly to these areas but the consideration of how to teach them enabled us to move away from a film production process which mirrors the industry model and towards a more playful and experimental approach. At times this came close to "So how do you do this?" followed by "Well let's try it and see." Rather than position themselves as 'expert' filmmakers who can potentially be overly directorial, Lovebytes filmmakers worked in closer proximity to the children's understanding: that is to say, asking questions, challenging ideas, suggesting alternative ways of doing things, and sometimes – most importantly perhaps – answering questions by saying "Well what do you think?" As a consequence we have interesting data about the role of the filmmaker and children's learning progression in response to distinct activities.

As we now approach the end of the project, the activities seem extensive in relation to other similarly funded projects. This, we would argue, is due to the lack of emphasis on one final film. Indeed we have made many, many films. At least 30 films of differing levels in terms of quality and completion; and using many different resources, ideas and technologies. Each reflects a different pedagogical approach which can be traced in the final texts. These include:

> Whole group pixilation (animation) of a box, chairs, bodies
> Stop frame animation with LEGO, paint, salt, objects
> 'Six shot' stories
> Editing
> Live action
> Documentary
> Trick shots

One group we worked with had been given a mission to create a 'six shot' film, carrying a large cardboard box downstairs. The planned focus of this group was close-up. One girl (Annie) took the role of filmmaker and, following a brief training session in which every child in the group had a camera, we moved quickly to filming. Once the children started filming going down the stairs we then remained upstairs out of shot, leaving the decision-making to the group and, in particular, to Annie. It was our plan that we would then look at this footage and ask the children how it could have been shot in a more interesting way. In the event, the short sequence they created was actually quite remarkable. Annie stopped the group from proceeding down the stairs in order to reposition herself, moving from a mid shot behind them to a tilt shot in front and below them on the stairs. She then instructed them to run past her and followed them with a pan. This sequence which we had expected to critically evaluate and then re-shoot was actually very dynamic and effective at first pass.

The box itself by then had become suggestive (it was used in a number of group projects in different ways). The children proposed making a film about what was in the box; they discussed a need to carry the box as if it was heavy; they began to invest the box with magical qualities and their ideas started to diverge considerably. We noted down every idea and explained we probably couldn't incorporate all of them; however this led to some strong reactions and disagreements. In the end we decided to impose some structure not by scripting, but by storyboarding, so the group devised the shots needed to tell the story and in this way a number of different ideas (aliens, zombies, spies) became intermingled. The storyboard helped shape a common story: three children entered a room unsuspectingly and one was hit by a falling box, zombies (aliens / spies) appeared and attacked the children and were then joined by their leader who had arrived in the box. The children's suggestions for shot types arose from their story ideas. So, for example, they wanted the box to appear from above so had to work out how best to shoot this. The group took turns to act and film so that every one of them took decisions about which shots to use, duration and other aspects of composition such as gesture and facial expressions.

At some point one of the group suggested using cameras as "weapons" which the other children felt was "random" (a good quality, apparently). As the film (now called *Paparazzi Invasion*) progressed this became a more significant element. The children had enjoyed being quite invasive, e.g. taking extreme close-ups of each other, during the camera training and this had prompted some discussion of what it might be like to be a celebrity. These ideas informed the children's choice of shots and the ending of their film. The final edit, with the sound of the camera whirring/clicking, did not convey all of the ideas the children intended. However, this also prompted a discussion about ambiguity – a film having many potential meanings or being unresolved.

During breaks this group chatted to us about the scrap store they had in the school playground. This was a new initiative in school, to encourage creative, imaginative and inclusive physical play and utilising recycled materials such as furniture, crates, costumes, old computers, crash mats etc. We, as adults, were very excited about what we observed but the children voiced some reservations in response. A key objection was the constraint this store placed on football and a slight sense that Year Six no longer ruled the roost!

We therefore planned the next session to enable them to make a documentary film about the scrap store and examine some of these ideas. Initially, the group planned some shot ideas and interviews and then we went out with three cameras including an iPad and an iPhone to film. They had to take it in turns to play with the materials and film each other. We asked those filming where they wanted the camera to be and what they wanted to film, encouraging them to direct each other. As a result we had a lot of footage which we then needed to shape. The organising idea for this came from the children's enthusiasm for a special effects app they had been shown, as well as the dominant ideas about risk and safety that were coming from the interviewees.

The children decided they wanted to film a sequence in which a meteor dropped on them in the playground, using the app. In the edit this was cut next to a member of staff saying how safe the playground was. They then filmed other sequences which suggested similar contrasts: e.g. one girl said "it is quiet" and this is followed by a shot from inside a barrel, in which a child was hurtling across the playground.

We interpret the data from this process to indicate that a playful approach to film production, which does not focus on the creation of one film, enables children to be more playful, to have a higher degree of creative autonomy over all aspects of the process, and to experiment. We would suggest that this is important because of the way it shifts focus from product and onto process, whilst recognising the importance to children of a finished film which will appeal to the audience. In fact this group made three films as a group and then six individual short films and this gave all of them the opportunity to extend their skills in terms of using aspects of film language. Connecting with the children's experiences was also significant to this process. Home and school and film and print were more permeable elements than might be assumed. We suggest that making these connections encourages children to recognise the possibility of independent filmmaking at home, a possibility we hope to explore further in a follow up project.

Finally, we observed that by enabling all children to train in the use of cameras, by ensuring all children undertook some filming and editing, and by giving them missions prior to them making their own films, we could see clear evidence of progression in terms of complex and purposeful decisions. Emerging evidence across all the groups we

Shot from inside a barrel

worked with suggests that, in order to increase participation in film production, children need regular opportunities to make film in school. Schools within a 'comprehensive' system provide spaces in which the playing field of opportunity can be levelled and it is critical we make arguments for more teacher training and curriculum space to support this. Far from being optional then, media literacy should take its central role within wider literacy teaching as an entitlement and should be enshrined in this form.

Underlying the 'mardy' tone of my title, which is also the name of the first Arctic Monkey's album (declaring my Sheffield allegiances), and referencing in turn the film *Saturday Night Sunday Morning* (enough said), is the desire to set the record straight about children, media and media education. In the current cold political climate, we have the proposal of a content-led, and frankly anachronistic primary curriculum which sidelines critical thinking, creativity and culture. Whilst this is hardly a surprise it should warrant greater concern and public debate. In the face of the constant use of education as a political football, collective action about curriculum would at the very least enable a wider range of voices to be heard. And those voices might just have something to say which is well-informed and mindful of the needs of contemporary children to examine and contribute to their own cultures and communities – online and off.

REFERENCES

Buckingham, D., Burn, A., Parry, B. and Powell, M. (2010) Minding the Gaps: Teachers' Cultures, Students' Cultures. In Alvermann, D. (ed.) *Adolescents' Online Literacies.* New York: Paul Lang.

Buckingham, D. and Sefton-Green, J. (1994) *Cultural Studies Goes to School: Reading And Teaching Popular Media.* London: Taylor and Francis.

Jenkins, H. et al. (2009) *Confronting the Challenges of Participatory Culture: Media Education for the 21st Century.* The J. D. and C. T. MacArthur Foundation Reports on Digital Media and Learning.

Kress, G. (1995) *Writing the Future: English and the Making of a Culture of Innovation.* Sheffield: NATE (National Association for the Teaching of English).

Lambirth, A. (2004) 'They get enough of that at home': Understanding aversion to popular culture in schools. Children's Literacy and Popular Culture, ESRC funded seminar series. 6th -11th February 2004, University of Sheffield (Available at http://wwwshef.ac.uk/content/1/c6/05/06/97/EG_11_2.pdf)

Lingard, B. (2005) Socially just pedagogies in changing times. In *International Studies in Sociology of Education*, Vol. 15, No. 2, July 2005, pp. 165-186.

Marsh, J. (2005) Ritual, Performance and Identity Construction: Young Children's Engagement with Popular Cultural and Media Texts. In Marsh, J. (ed.) *Popular Culture, New Media and Digital Literacy in Early Childhood.* Oxford: Routledge Falmer.

Pahl, K. (2006) Children's popular culture in the home: tracing children cultural practices in texts. In Marsh, J. and Millard, E. (eds) *Popular Literacies, Childhood and Schooling.* London: Routledge Falmer.

Parry, B. (2010) Helping Children Tell the Stories in their Heads. In Bazalgette, C. (ed.) *Teaching Media in Primary School.* London: Sage.

Willet, R. (2009) Young people's video productions as new sites of learning. In Carrington, V. and Robinson, M. (eds) *Digital Literacies: Social Learning and Classroom Practices.* London: Sage.

Williams, R. (1989) *Raymond Williams on Television: Selected Writings.* New York: Routledge.

--------- NOTES --------------------

1. http://www.esrc.ac.uk/my-esrc/grants/RES-062-23-1292/read

Illustration by An Vrombaut

Media education
Researching new literacy at home at school and in between

John Potter

As we head towards the middle of the second decade of the 21st century, we find the dominant mode of cultural expression - the moving image - along with social and other new media forms, marginalised or absent in the school curriculum in England. And yet, as other developed and developing countries recognise, such media forms are part of everyday, lived experience and could perhaps be accounted for by broadening our conception of literacy. In these systems, as well as in the eyes of many commentators, the ability to manage the media we consume, to make sense of the vast and multiple sources of information we sift through and to construct and share all kinds of personal media texts, is something desirable and even essential. Clearly it is no longer sensible, or even tenable, to think of learning about print literacy as the sole focus of education.

One question we could ask is: how do we proceed to broaden and redefine literacy in a system in which many teachers have themselves been made to feel marginalised and de-professionalised? Another pair of questions are: how, and in what spaces within the school, can we introduce critical work with media, including production, when the narrow, fossilised vision of literacy – as a set of technical skills disconnected from culture – persists? Finally: where is the research to back up any assertions about the methods and benefits of media education?

A series of projects which I have either seen reported or been personally involved with in recent years, gives rise to cautious optimism about how some of these questions might be answered. Here are some examples:

Two boys aged about thirteen describing a video game they have authored from the raw material of Act one, Scene five of *Macbeth*, which took some of the tropes of games, e.g. the ammo meter, and changed them for "conscience meter" etc., creating new interpretations of the text in new media;

A school in a rural area in which children as young as six learn the value of working with poetry and animation together – two simultaneously time and image based forms supporting each other;

Students from a school in central London involved with film-making, learning a high-aesthetic form of media language with a filmmaker and teacher but incorporating their own cultural capital and interests in their work and defending its aesthetic form and choices made during its production;

Two schools in the North and South of England respectively, which reveal that, far from being extinct, the playground game is alive and well and, as ever, incorporating new popular cultural forms;

Working with a doctoral student who is looking at the very start of media language in the viewing habits and practices of her grandchildren.

Some of the work listed above is reported on the website of the DARE research collaborative (Digital, Arts, Research, Education at www.darecollaborative.net) and it has a life on several other partner sites and in pages of reports and papers. But, beyond the essential reportage, it has a life through the quality of the experiences for the participants, as well as in the media texts which were made.

What are the shared characteristics of these projects and practices? I think they all, in some way, reflect the belief that media are part of everyday, lived culture and experience and that – in the right circumstances – they can have a productive and engaging relationship with learning and teaching. The difference between them, in many cases, were the surrounding organisational factors, which sometimes depended on after-school time or increased staffing or a special, externally funded project. But many were compatible with, and can map onto, a set of enriching learning experiences, particularly across the boundary between home and school.

How do we proceed? Partly as a result of thinking about these issues, I wrote a version of a manifesto for media education (one of several at www.manifestoformediaeducation. co.uk) which addresses them in the form of nine principles, the first three of which are:

> Firstly, and most obviously, we need to look at widening the conception and definition of literacy so that we think about the screen-based modes of cultural production alongside print and think about what it truly means to be literate in the new media age;

> Secondly, in doing this, there is a pressing need to connect with the lives of learners in a curriculum based around the 'what' and the 'how' of the media that is made, shared, consumed, interpreted, and exhibited in lived culture;

> The third principle involves dialogue with learners about their experiences, skills and dispositions in the uses of media in all settings. This will support us in thinking of ways in which young children can learn about time-based texts, and how the modes of gesture, image, speech, and music can be made to produce specific meanings in these forms, from the earliest years.

The final principle recognised that we all - adults, young people and children - are living in a world in which the media we collect and make can be organised, displayed, and re-presented time and again in ways that were not possible before. This 'curatorship of the self' is a new form of cultural production that is pitched partway between making and sharing, creating temporary collections for specific purposes, and then dismantling them again. Should we not recognise this - and the skills, knowledge and dispositions which go with it - as a practice and build from there?

It's apparent that we need much more research in the field which demonstrates added value from media production as well as acknowledging those things which do not always work. Celebratory reporting has its place but research which takes full account of the setting and tries to locate, hear and contextualise the voices of teachers and learners will be of more lasting value. Researchers can and should be partners with teachers and learners investigating productive agency with media at home, at school and in the spaces between.

Illustration by Nick Mackie

this page

Waste of time or vital learning? 19

Cary Bazalgette

The first page of the 47 million plus results for a Google search on "toddlers and TV" contains the words "guidelines", "harm", "risk", "negative", "too much" and questions such as "is TV right for toddlers?" and "should you let your toddler watch TV?" But searching for the same topic on advice websites - even those from the USA like babycenter.com or babyshrink.com - shows up rather more balanced views, while online parental discussions on this topic, for example at mumsnet.com or netmums, are full of posts like, "My LO [little one] always used to have cbeebies on in the morning. Now she is more interested in programs what have got animals in like vet programmes or planets funniest animals (she loves animals!) I don't mind her watching tele as long as she isn't sitting in front of it all day."

So what's going on here? The Google search shows that lots of people must be thinking about risk and harm when they search for online information about toddlers and TV, but, at the same time, parents are gratefully turning on the TV for their babies and toddlers, and later on buying them TV sets for their bedrooms (or, more likely, putting the old one up there when they upgrade the living room one). Yet when I tell people that I am doing research on children and television (and film), they often ask, "So have you found out how if affects them?" or, more directly, "What's your point of view: is it good for them or bad for them?"

I'm bored with the 'is it bad for them or not' debate. What interests me, is that, pretty much without being taught how to, children understand stories in television programmes and films by the time they are four. I think this is an amazing feat of independent learning by very young children, and something quite new in human history. After all, it's only about 30 years since the home VCR made it possible for all of us – including toddlers – to re-view bits of film and TV over and over again. Most people with children have stories about their kids doing this. Some people worry about it, but others – including me – recognise that there must be something important and useful for the child in this activity, or they wouldn't be doing it.

My hunch is that children are attentive to TV and films even before they can understand much of them, because they recognise that these are meaningful forms that are important to all of us, and they *want* to understand them – just as they recognise that spoken language is a vital part of human life and they must learn it. I'm not suggesting that moving-image media are as important as verbal language – of course not – but I am pointing out that the 'language' of moving images and sounds is something that we learn. We learn it very easily, and we learn it very early, but we do learn it, and we learn it on our own.

These media aren't transparent windows on the world: they have their own very particular ways of making meaning. Close-ups, jump cuts, editing techniques like cutaways, shot/reverse shot and parallel montage, are different from the ways we experience the real world; yet they are devices that everybody understands, even if few of us could actually name them. The same goes for added sounds like commentaries or music. Animation introduces entirely different ways of presenting characters and telling stories, yet it is animation that very young children watch most.

So what I am trying to do, in my doctoral research at the Institute of Education in London, is to develop new theory about how very young children learn to make sense of television and film. Taking my own twin grandchildren as a focus, I'm using observations, video and interviews to build up a picture of what goes on between the ages of eighteen months and three and a half, as children watch TV programmes, DVDs, YouTube videos and games, and adapt them to fuel their own stories, games and thinking. It's fascinating, but quite a challenge, given that my work sits at the intersection of several very different academic disciplines.

I've come to this late in life: I spent 27 years in the British Film Institute's Education Department, developing curricula, teaching resources and teacher training for learning about moving-image media in schools, and trying to make the case to Government for the value of this kind of learning. The teachers I met were always amazed at its impact and potential, not only as a support and stimulus for conventional literacy, but also as an obviously important part of life in the 21st century. Policymakers were more cautious: they feared the headlines about teachers wasting time on television in the classroom. After all, we all know that television is a waste of time – don't we?

Digital Media and the Everyday Lives of Young Children

Lydia Plowman

Finding out about Children and Digital Media

Many people believe that children need to become competent users of digital media to avoid disadvantage or marginalisation and to become discriminating and effective members of society. For others, the ubiquity of these technologies has led to concerns about the ways in which they are seen to exert influence on the lives of young children. Like it or not, most people would agree that children's experiences with technology – whether for play, learning, or communication – will have significant implications for their future lives. How dominant is technology in children's lives and what do parents think about this? What kinds of things do three and four year old children like to do and what do they like to play with? How important is it for parents to feel confident that their children are learning when they are playing with digital media? Our research into play, learning and technology in the everyday lives of young children sets out to answer some of these questions.

Our approach to studying these questions requires detailed documentation of everyday lives and of children's play with a range of domestic, leisure and work technologies, including interactive toys. Depending on the specific question we're interested in, we collect information in different ways: children taking photos and telling us about their favourite toys and activities; parents telling us about their perceptions of their child's play and learning; surveys of toys and technologies at home; detailed analysis of video recordings of children's interactions with interactive toys and websites; family interviews about the transition to school at age five; and others too.

What are Children Using?

In addition to access to technological toys and digital games, preschoolers also used computers, smartphones and iPods that were attractive to them but designed for adults.

All had at least one interactive learning toy such as a VTech or LeapFrog play laptop or console. In line with our findings, Ofcom data from 2012 shows that many in the three to four age group are using different media devices, including over a third who are going online using a desktop PC, laptop or netbook and 6% who are going online via a tablet computer.[1] Although the number of preschool children using tablets such as iPads is currently low, we expect it to increase rapidly as tablets are a source of games, videos and stories and are used by parents to occupy children on car journeys. Our most recent research suggests that children who are used to interacting with a tablet have problems using a mouse as an input device and that this is something that designers will need to take into account.

Ofcom data also show that the majority (97%) of three to four year olds watch television programmes on a TV set, but 18% have also watched programmes on devices such as a PC, laptop or netbook (12%), a games console or player (7%), and on a tablet computer (6%). Our data diverges from Ofcom's, however, in the number of children who had a television in their bedroom: Ofcom states that a third of children did, whereas in our study this was about 10%. Like Ofcom, we found that nearly all parents claim to regulate their child's access to television and computers.

However, children's experiences of using digital media varied considerably. Parents' values and attitudes to learning and the perceived benefits of technology shape household practices more than the number of digital products or household income. Children's own interests, which develop and change quite frequently, influenced use: some were keen to play with the latest devices, while others preferred traditional toys and chose these even when others at home were digital enthusiasts. Children had a wide range of play preferences at home and in their preschool settings and extensive supplies of traditional toys for use inside and outdoors as well as access to digital media and playthings, some shared with other family members and some designed specifically for preschool children.

Interest in using digital media to support children's learning increased as school became imminent but not all parents were concerned about this: some thought that there was plenty of time for a focus on learning once their child was at school. Our mobile phone diaries showed that parents described about a quarter of children's activities at weekends as play or playing.[2] Roughly 10% of the total responses made references to technological play, although watching television was not usually categorised as such. Overall, parents were concerned with outdoor play; encouraging time with family and friends; providing both traditional and technological playthings; and ensuring a balance of activities for their children.

Play and Learning

Parents and other relatives purchase interactive learning toys in the belief that they will help their child's education, although most toys, whether traditional or electronic, could be described as educational in one way or another, especially if a parent or sibling joins in. Although parents seem to succumb quite readily to marketing based on educational value, they also voice the view that they would prefer their child to be having fun and enjoying themselves at home rather than trying to achieve particular learning outcomes.

Play value is important in the early years. Children do not generally ask for these toys or use these products for the purpose of supporting their learning: they choose them if they are fun to play with. Websites or apps that claim some learning content may be more successful: the outlay is minimal and children usually respond positively to being able to choose games featuring characters that they are familiar with from favourite television programmes.

However, the interactive learning toys do not have a monopoly on mundane tasks and limited concepts of learning: we find these in the websites and apps designed for children, too. Reading, writing and understanding numbers are complex sets of skills that develop over a period of time, but these interactive products are often based on a restricted view of learning as a sequence of easily identifiable skills which can be broken down into discrete, testable elements. Many of the interactive learning toys, websites and apps promote a limited form of functional literacy that is more concerned with letter sounds and word recognition than an expansive form of literacy which involves the children's own storytelling, pleasure in words, and access to the world of the imagination and communication. While some children enjoy these activities and the repetition involved, others soon find them rather tedious (we didn't come across children who wanted to get a head start on phonics) and might prefer more imaginative play. Products with the functionality to offer a wider range of activities and the opportunity for children to insert their own photos, drawings and voice may be more successful in this regard, although there may be a trade-off with how easy they are to use.

Overall, we found no reason to suggest that children's wellbeing is threatened by digital media. Parents usually know what's best for their own children and feel reasonably comfortable about the decisions they make and, at this stage in their children's lives, the domestic management of technology is not a major concern. With the proviso that quality content and design is paramount, there is potential for digital media to extend the possibilities for children's learning and to transform our expectations of what children of this age have the capacity to do. The big 'but' is the need for better design.

Design

With some exceptions, neither interaction design nor content design currently serves the interests of children of this age as much as is desirable. The many products, apps and websites that aim to support learning draw on models of learning that are often narrow, naïve and outdated. Current educational thinking sees early learning as more than the development of intellectual processes: it includes changes in the ways in which children participate in the world around them and how they learn to interact with people and objects with increased competence and independence. This expanded way of thinking about learning is rarely seen in products designed for young children.

We need to take design seriously if we want to promote curiosity, creativity and an enthusiasm for learning. We also need to recognise the importance of foregrounding joy, pleasure, fun, play and excitement – it's not all about structured learning activities. Children are not just adults-in-training or mini versions of bigger children. So when we're designing technologies for children in the early years it's important to find out what's suitable. There is an enormous spectrum of dispositions, skills and competences even within a single year of a child's life at this stage but, for typically developing preschool children, we tend to underestimate their capacity for learning while overestimating the extent to which they can get to grips with an unfamiliar and poorly designed interface: children need guidance and support from others and from good design.[3] We need to understand that learning in the early years is about relationships; so products need to be designed for sharing – with parents, siblings, other family members, teachers and friends – as well as functioning for the independent user. We need innovative products that open up possibilities for new forms of interaction and from designers who recognise how young children learn, create and communicate.

Because we looked at the big picture of children's everyday lives, we found that technology does not dominate or hinder social interaction in the ways suggested by media coverage. Beliefs that there is a natural affinity between children and technology or that children of this age are more tech savvy than grown-ups also seemed to be unfounded.[4] Although parents occasionally expressed some disquiet about the role of technology, families made choices concerning preschoolers' play and other activities based on their own values and circumstances and did not consider children's education, socialisation or wellbeing to be under threat.

This summary is based on several research projects, with colleagues including Joanna McPake and Christine Stephen, which have focused on young children and their uses of digital media at home and in preschool settings. Funders have included the Economic and Social Research Council, the BBC and Which? *magazine. A list of projects can be found at* www.ed.ac.uk/education/lydia-plowman *and, from there, links to a wide range of downloadable publications for academic audiences and others, including the ones noted here.*

--------- Notes --------------------

1. Ofcom (2012) *Children and Parents: Media Use and Attitudes Report*. 23rd October 2012.

2. Plowman, L. and Stevenson, O. (2012) Using mobile phones to explore children's everyday lives. *Childhood*, Vol. 19, No.4, pp 539-553.

3. Plowman, L. (2012) *Press for Play: Using technology to enhance learning in the early years*. London: ESRC Technology Enhanced Learning Research Programme.

4. Plowman, L. and McPake, J. (2013) Seven Myths About Young Children and Technology. *Childhood Education*, Vol. 89, No. 1, pp 27-33.

Illustration by Evgenia Golubeva

Children's TV and the Rise and Fall of the Preschool Content Specialist

Jeanette Steemers

With hits like *Teletubbies* and *Bob the Builder* in the 1990s and, more recently, *Peppa Pig* and *Tree Fu Tom,* one small sector of the UK children's production market - preschool television - has proved remarkably successful in terms of exports and international acclaim. These are all programmes made by British independents and aired on public service broadcasting (PSB) channels, foremost the BBC, but including Five (*Peppa Pig*) since the mid-1990s. In fact, with the emergence of dedicated children's channels, particularly CBeebies in 2002, the UK preschool sector was transformed from an essentially domestic enterprise linked to public service broadcasting into one that is now much more international, but still strongly connected to PSB.

This has occurred in spite of global market domination by three of the world's largest media conglomerates – Disney, Time Warner and Viacom - who not only own or part-own most of the dedicated children's channels worldwide, but who are expert at leveraging their own content across children's entertainment and consumer products. These players rarely commission or broadcast local content, relying instead on their own US-originated animation or sitcoms (D'Arma and Steemers, 2012). This leaves PSBs as the main funders and outlets for homegrown children's television. In the UK, the BBC transmits high levels of domestic content (including repeats). It has become the dominant commissioner since 2006 when ITV drastically reduced production investment following the removal of production quotas in the Communications Act 2003, reinforced by a ban, in 2007, on advertising for foods high in sugar, fat and salt in children's airtime.

With shrinking budgets and over 30 children's channels battling for UK audiences, co-production and revenues from licensed merchandise are now key to recouping investment, even for quite modestly budgeted live-action programmes. Securing funding is especially daunting during recession. The importance of consumer products also blurs public service and commercial priorities as attention is focused on a more limited range of commercially and internationally appealing character-based animation, rather than drama or factual programmes or programmes featuring 'real' people, which are less attractive for international sales or commercial exploitation by toy companies and retailers (Steemers, 2010). However, without licensing revenues some British preschool shows could not be made, because domestic broadcasters only cover a very small proportion of the budget, often not more than 10% for animation. With long lead times of up to five years before revenues come on stream, this tends to favour larger producers and toy manufacturers (e.g. Mattel, Hasbro) who can afford to wait, thus leaving fewer opportunities for smaller content producers. Finally there are the pressures of changing consumption habits (hypercompetition) as children migrate to media content and applications on other platforms including tablets, although, *for the time being*, children's TV consumption remains pretty stable at about 2.5 hours a day (Ofcom, 2012a).

If we examine hours of children's output in the UK there is no market failure in terms of quantity, but UK originations are rather thin on the ground, and the BBC commissions most of these. This puts it in a very powerful position over the production community, raising questions about choice, creative competition, plurality of provision and the future health of PSB children's output. Since 2004, PSB expenditure on first-run originations has fallen from £139m to £88m in 2011; during the same timespan, PSB first-run hours of originations dropped from 1887 hours to 777 hours (Ofcom, 2012b).

Such a picture lies in stark contrast to the one that emerged in the 1990s and early 2000s. During this period a small number of British rights-owning production-distribution companies became involved in the creation and brand management of their own preschool brands. They included HIT Entertainment, Chorion and Entertainment Rights. These companies established a model for funding and marketing preschool television, based largely on global ancillary rights exploitation (licensed merchandise) of character-based properties. Supported initially by stock market launches, a key motivation was the satisfaction of shareholders and investors. HIT Entertainment, in particular, served for a time as a template for other UK players. Over 90% of HIT's revenues came from consumer products and home entertainment (DVDs) (Steemers

2010). Driven by acquisitions (*Thomas the Tank Engine, Barney*) it targeted the lucrative US market. In 2011 HIT was sold by private equity firm Apax to toy company Mattel, following a lean period in which it was hit by declining DVD sales and competition from larger, integrated US companies with their own channels.

Other medium-sized producers copied the model developed by HIT, because UK broadcasters were paying less or virtually nothing for content. Companies sold programming at low cost to broadcasters in order to generate awareness for consumer products, but this only works if you have a hit. This made companies vulnerable when the recession hit. Some companies did not survive. Entertainment Rights collapsed under the strain of servicing debts incurred from spending too much on acquiring properties or investing in programming that did not generate enough revenues. In 2011, Chorion, the company behind *Noddy, Mr Men* and *Octonauts*, was forced to sell most of its brands, having hit financial difficulties. In November 2012, Chapman Entertainment, producers of *Fifi and the Flowertots* and *Little Charlie Bear*, became the latest casualty of a difficult trading environment when it entered administration. The strategy of focusing on consumer product revenues might have been logical in the context of globalising tendencies in the children's market, but it was also flawed because of limited access to US distribution platforms (broadcast channels) through which to drive product sales, and because of underlying structural and financial weaknesses that were revealed once the recession started to bite.

The practical reality is that the economics of homegrown children's television are now even more unattractive for producers, forcing many to question the old model of broadcast commissions and to consider other revenue-generating possibilities from shortform content and applications which can be accessed online or on mobiles or tablets. The introduction of animation tax breaks in 2013 could stimulate UK animation, attract external investment from the likes of Disney, and hopefully reverse the trend for outsourcing production to the Far East and countries with production tax breaks such as Canada and Ireland. However, if focusing solely on animation, the tax breaks cannot address broader PSB goals for a wide range of domestic content for children.

REFERENCES

D'Arma, A. and Steemers, J. (2012) Localisation Strategies of US-owned Children's Television Networks in Five European Markets. *Journal of Children and the Media*, Vol. 6, No. 2, pp 147-163.

Ofcom (2012a) *Children and Parents: Media Use and Attitudes Report* http://stakeholders.ofcom.org.uk/binaries/research/media-literacy/oct2012/main.pdf, 23 October 2012

Ofcom (2012b) *Public Service Broadcasting: Annual Report 2012* http://stakeholders.ofcom.org.uk/broadcasting/reviews-investigations/public-service-broadcasting/annrep/psb12/

Steemers, J. (2010) *Creating Preschool Television: A Story of Commerce, Creativity and Curriculum*. London: Palgrave.

Based on a talk originally given at the Cowboys or Indies? Arts and Humanities Research Council (AHRC) funded conference, National Film Theatre, 20 September 2012.

'Make up your favourite TV host' 22
Discussion of the UK element of a global study on children's television presenters
Alexandra Swann

Mr Tumble, Steve Backshall, Helena Dowling: these are the presenters that children engage with every week, sometimes every day. These presenters guide children through the show, pointing them towards interesting facts and explaining complicated points. Children identify with these individuals (Hoffner and Buchanan, 2009; Götz, 2010), tending to prefer presenters of the same gender and ethnic background as themselves (Hoffner, 2005; Götz, 2009; Götz, 2010). IZI (the International Central Institute for Youth and Educational Television) put together an international study in 2012 with the aim of investigating seven to ten year olds' perceptions of children's television presenters and of re-examining the existing view that children do indeed prefer presenters of the same gender and ethnicity as themselves. Almost 3,000 (2,839) children from 24 countries took part. The findings of the UK-based element will be discussed here.

A total of 448 children took part in the UK study, divided equally between boys and girls. 70 Scottish children, 94 English and 284 children from Northern Ireland were recruited from schools. Teachers and/or the researchers administered the study which consisted of two parts. The first part consisted of a quantitative survey investigating what children want in a television presenter. Participants were provided with a page of images representing a range of characteristics of a presenter's appearance and were asked to indicate their preferences. The images represented age, gender, body shape, whether they wore glasses, skin colour and hair colour. Using the selections, they would build up an image of their ideal presenter, an individual framed as "a presenter for a children's TV show who discovers new and exciting things with you". Next, children were asked to turn the page over and build up a portrait of themselves using the same images and selection categories. While such approach dealt purely with external physicalities therefore (and not personality or other such characteristics), it was considered to be an effective means of mapping broad preferences within a large-scale international study in which there may be no common presenter-led programme texts. The researchers absolutely acknowledge the limitations of such an approach for an assessment of the specific or likely appeal of particular presenters in particular contexts. Likewise it is acknowledged that the study was not designed to look at aspects of physical disability.

The second part of the study required participants to consider a television programme from which they had learned something and to draw a scene from this. The drawing was supported by a short description of what the programme was and what the child felt they had learned from it. The qualitative element of the study followed on from the first section, together comprising a single session lasting approximately 45 minutes. The activities had a certain amount of conceptual overlap: the children's choice of a presenter was therefore linked to the idea that television could be a learning tool and that the presenter can act as a "learning companion".

Ideal television presenter

The majority of children from the UK sample wanted a presenter who was the same gender, appearance and ethnicity as them. This reflected the findings of the global sample. 85% of boys and 76% of girls from the UK wanted a presenter of the same gender as themselves. Three children (0.7%) from the UK specifically stated they wanted both genders; nonetheless the evidence overwhelmingly supports that children prefer presenters to be of the same gender as themselves.

The majority of children from the UK (46%) wanted to see a presenter who was a young adult (although it should be noted that the category of "young adult" had no specific age attached but instead was placed between "teen" and "adult"). We found that there was no significant difference in the responses of the younger and older children of our sample, or between boys and girls.

The ideal presenter has blue eyes, dark hair and light skin (the researchers like to think of him as CBBC's Ed Petrie). Participants preferred a presenter of slim to average weight. Children with grey or green eyes, or who identified themselves as in the heavier body shape categories, did not want to see these characteristics onscreen in a children's television presenter (though it should be stressed again that the survey did not attempt in any way to look at children's preferences for *actual* presenters).

Skin colour was represented by means of a shade chart. The majority (57%) of darker or black skinned children in the UK sample wanted darker or black skinned presenters; this was a higher percentage than that of the global sample (40%). Generally, in our sample, light skinned children preferred presenters with light skin, but 17% of children with light skin wanted presenters with darker or black skins. One might speculate that the higher number of the UK sample compared to the global sample could suggest one of two things: 1) that diversity policies in UK programming – in particular by the BBC – is having a positive effect on perceptions; or 2) that children perceive a particular 'lack' in these representations and so wish to see more of them. Of course, with this sort of research instrument it was not possible to assess whether children like what they get and therefore vote to maintain the status quo or can imagine a presenter who is genuinely outwith the norms. The research set-up did try to emphasise that children should be free to 'think outside the box' but whether this was, or can be achieved, is debatable.

Within our UK sample, 80% of children were Caucasian. The majority of children who identified with Caucasian, Asian, Chinese or East Asian and Black ethnicities wanted a Caucasian presenter. Almost half (45%) of the children who identified with the Middle Eastern group wanted a Middle Eastern presenter. Several children objected to stating a preference for the ethnicity of the presenter, or noted that it did not matter; several children also refused to answer or be 'positioned' by the study in this way; and several children indicated - on paper or verbally to the researchers - that they felt the question to be "racist" in that it asked for a preference at all. Other questions of 'pointless preference' also frustrated some children and therefore additional categories of "don't care" or "don't mind" or "doesn't matter" were spontaneously inserted by children into the questionnaires: we saw this repeatedly on the question as to whether or not the presenter should wear glasses. As such responses were not inserted into questions of e.g. hair and eye colour, it could be inferred that children only felt frustrated in the instances where they felt the question was particularly 'loaded' towards intolerance.

The pictures drawn by the UK children, in the second half of the research exercise, demonstrated the diversity of genres and learning experiences that they encountered while watching television. From 448 children we were given 151 different programme names across every conceivable format: quiz shows, adult dramas and soaps, sports coverage, feature films, news and documentary and wildlife shows, as well as children's content of every shape and size. Children's content accounted for 70% of all texts cited, with family-orientated content accounting for a further 20% and adult content accounting for 7%.

Boy, 9, UK

I learned weird and wacky facts about historical eras like a fraction of the German army were pensioners and toothpaste used to made of butter, sugar and gunpowder.

Boy, 9, UK

I have drawn a little boy and his dad taking part in a DNA test because the boy didn't think his dad was his real dad. They are waiting for a phone call from the DNA people. I learned that science can prove if you are related or not.

In the UK, every fourth child named a cartoon series as a programme from which they have learned something. *SpongeBob SquarePants* was the individual text with the most citations (49). Knowledge-centred shows and factual formats occupied a similar share, with *Horrible Histories* (30) and *Deadly 60* (34) being especially popular. Children were keen to relate in detail the facts they had learned from these types of series or factual formats, such as the ten year old boy who noted he had learned that "a type of toad can eat only with its eyes". Interestingly, although these and other BBC texts such as *Frozen Planet*, *BBC News* and *Top Gear* were stand out citations, the distribution between public service and commercial platforms was equal over all and children did not necessarily distinguish 'television' texts proper from e.g. films shown on television (a good example of this is the child who cited the 1970 WW2 film *Kelly's Heroes*). Around one-fifth of children indicated they had gained practical skills in areas such as art, sport, music, and mathematics, by copying what they had seen on knowledge-centred programmes.

Knowledge and facts aside, and again bearing in mind that *SpongeBob* was the single most cited text, it is interesting to note that children frequently indicated that appropriate

Boy, 9, UK
A type of toad can eat only with its eyes.

Child, 8, UK
I learned how to catch jellyfish

social relations was what they learned from a text. Children felt prosocial behaviour such as sharing and practising had been promoted in television programmes, and themes relevant to valuing family and friends were often cited: indeed the importance of friendship was the single most reported 'learning experience' associated with *SpongeBob*. It should be noted that the researchers suspected there was a certain amount of 'retro-fitting' of learning messages onto programmes and characters that children especially liked and *felt able to draw*: the relative ease in drawing, may in part, count for the popularity of *SpongeBob* within the responses.

Conclusion

Both parts of the UK element of this global study on children's television presenters yielded results that could have positive conclusions relating to children's perceptions of ethnicity and skin colour, as well as the range of television programmes with which they engage. Regarding the former, children in the UK with light coloured and dark coloured skin (according to the shade chart) were more comfortable seeing darker or black skinned presenters than their counterparts in the global sample. Indeed, a number took the time to write on the questionnaire that they did not consider this to be an important factor. This positive conclusion is tentative however as the study was not designed to deal with actual instances of preference. Nonetheless the findings offer conclusive evidence that children on the whole wish to see their own gender and ethnicity reflected in an ideal presenter. The researchers would urge particular caution in the way that this might be interpreted by the production community: it should reinforce a need for diversity, not the reverse. Indeed, challenge to the status quo would seem a particular thrust of IZI's mission.

The qualitative element of the study highlighted that children have decided opinions about what they watch; they are enriched by their time in front of the screen, and recognise this: they are as happy to point to the 'soft' learning benefits of narrative as to the more obvious pedagogic learning aspects. Children did not distinguish between PSB or commercial content, indicating that they see learning opportunities in each. They were just as likely to list dramas, whether live-action or animated (and including soaps and other non-children's formats) as they were to list the more obvious learning formats such as factual shows. Every time they watch a television show, they are prepared to learn.

Illustration by An Vrombaut

{ Farewell }

John Coates 1927-2012

Paul Madden

I first met John when he came into my office at Channel 4 in December 1981 to show me an animatic based on a Raymond Briggs book which he wanted to make into a film. That was *The Snowman*.

With his trademark twinkling eyes, unquenchable optimism and rotund good cheer, John was not unlike Raymond's Father Christmas character. A legend in his own lunchtime and far beyond – one birthday celebration for John at Elena's L'Etoile lasted from noon until almost midnight, the longest birthday party lunch Elena swore she'd ever hosted.

After *The Snowman* we worked together on five or so films including *Granpa*, *Famous Fred*, and *The Bear* (and more we couldn't get funded) and had lots of good times on the way, in Sussex, Soho, Fitzrovia, Annecy, LA and, er, Cardiff, unfailingly topped or tailed by lashings of red wine or champagne.

In its 30 years, Channel 4 has shown the film every Christmas but one (when a video version was released with a David Bowie introduction). And no one can escape 'Walking in the Air' during the festive season.

British animation has lost one of its iconic figures, and we'll all miss him, but Christmas wouldn't be complete without *The Snowman*, John's enduring legacy to every generation.

Wendy Duggan 1928-2012

Paul R. Jackson

Former Animal Advisor to the BBC Children's Department from 1965-98, Wendy Duggan died on 20th February 2012, aged 84.

Wendy had studied photography and, during the sixties, worked as an assistant to the great fashion and portrait photographer, Sir Cecil Beaton; this role introduced her to a world of celebrities and royals, and she attended the wedding of Lord Snowdon to Princess Margaret in 1960. Wendy's uncle was a vet and bred birds and it was this that gave Wendy her lifelong interest in the species, later gaining a zoology degree and, in 1976, becoming a Fellow of the Zoological Society. Wendy was employed by Joy Whitby, founding producer of *Play School*, in 1965 and stayed with the programme until it ended in 1988, providing all the resident and visiting pets, including K'too the cockatoo (who lived with her). She was known affectionately by both presenters and production team as "Pets" Wendy and used her many contacts to provide many types of animals to generations of producers.

I first met Wendy in the early 1980s when I joined the BBC and was honoured to be invited as her guest to the wrap party after the final *Play School* in March 1988 and after I left the BBC we kept in touch. Wendy sadly suffered a stroke in 2007 yet still helped with contacts and stories for my publications. In 2008 she celebrated her 40th wedding anniversary to Ron Riches. Wendy kept in touch with former school friend, actress Penelope Keith, and, through her BBC connections, was friends with many actors including John Le Mesurier, James Beck and Tony Hancock. On one occasion Hancock, who shared her love for animals, insisted on accompanying her to Charing Cross hospital, where she was overseeing the x-raying of rabbits to show children that the process was not harmful. He brought the radiology department down with laughter.

Wendy's funeral took place at Putney Vale cemetery on March 5th 2012 and was attended by many former colleagues from the BBC Children's Department and current Director of BBC Children's, Joe Godwin.

Clive Dunn, OBE 1920-2012

Jeremy Swan

Clive Dunn illuminated two television series for BBC with his comic genius – *Dad's Army* as Lance Corporal Jones for Light Entertainment, and *Grandad* as Charlie Quick for Children's, which I produced.

Clive was a joy to work with. His inherited theatrical talent made him an inescapable attraction for the audience, as a naughty and playful old man with all the capriciousness of a mischievous child. With Bob Block's scripts he made the character a person to whom the viewer could instantly relate.

Clive and I would work a long day on each script to hone every line for the biggest laughs – which were always achieved from the studio audience.

He gave me a friendship which I cherish with his wife, Priscilla, and his daughters, Polly and Jessica, and his own grandchildren, Alice and Lydia.

I went to a memorial party for Clive in Portugal where they all live; the tributes and affection from that gathering emphasised that he was a dear, exceptional and funny man, a good friend, a beloved husband, a wonderful father and the perfect Grandad who will always stay in our memories.

John MA (Marshall Austin) Lane 1933-2012

Paul R. Jackson

Known affectionately as "Leathers" Lane (due to his love of riding motorbikes), former BBC Children's producer/director/writer died, after a long battle with cancer, on 24th December 2012, aged 79.

John had previously worked in the West End with director Peter Hall then went off for six months to be a gaucho in South America before returning to the theatre. He worked on the original productions of *Waiting for Godot* at the Arts Theatre Club and on *Oliver!* starring Barry Humphries as Fagan, and was headhunted to join the BBC in studio management in 1963. He worked as Floor Manager on the first *Jackanory* in December 1965 and joined the Children's Dept in 1966. In 1968 he began a seventeen year association with *Play School* and later directed for three years on the *Multi-coloured Swap Shop* outside broadcast. He later moved to Further Education as a Senior Producer.

He retired in 1987 and afterwards worked as a freelance director on many episodes of the popular European daytime quiz, *Going for Gold*, at Elstree Studios.

Terry Nutkins 1946-2012

Marshall Corwin

I spent my last weekend with Terry – and his fellow TV presenter Chris Rogers – in unusually beautiful weather at his remote cottage on the North West coast of Scotland.

He had just been diagnosed with a rare and acute form of leukaemia and it seemed appropriate to be surrounded by everything he loved: friends, family, animals, food, beer – and the most spectacular view across the Sound of Sleat to Skye. This extraordinary, wild and spiritual place was inextricably linked to Terry throughout his life.

As a child he had had the most unconventional and tough upbringing just a few miles along the coast, helping the author Gavin Maxwell bring up three otters, a story immortalised in the bestselling book and film *Ring of Bright Water*. Terry was irresistibly drawn back to this magical place to live and, eventually, die.

He had a huge love of life and an almost mystical connection with nature and animals. Even when one of the otters he looked after bit off part of a finger on each hand, he didn't blame the animal at all, just his own stupidity in reaching out to the otter while holding a cardigan full of the scent of a visitor to the cottage.

Terry's childhood reads like a fictional adventure story. He lived in central London but at the age of eight started to play truant from school, heading instead to London Zoo, where he climbed over the walls of the elephant enclosure to be with the animals. Remarkably the huge creatures never turned on him, and Terry described how he would avoid washing his hands when he went to bed as he loved the smell of the animals so much. The keepers recognised that they had a very unusual child on their hands and made Terry the founder member of the XYZ Club (the Extraordinary Young Zoologists), giving him the job of mucking out the enclosures.

When Gavin Maxwell approached the zoo for a young assistant to help look after his otters over the summer holidays, Terry was the natural choice, and at the age of eleven he was packed off on a steam train 600 miles north to a completely different world. He ended up staying there through the rest of his childhood.

"I loved it up there with the dolphins, the basking sharks, eagles, pine martins and everything out there in the wild," he explained. "I wouldn't see people for months: it was just the otters and Gavin and me."

Terry's other great mentor was Johnny Morris, the brilliant presenter of the hugely popular BBC1 show *Animal Magic*. Terry made his TV debut on the programme with a sea lion called Gemini, which he had hand-reared in Scotland after it was abandoned by its mother. Terry was a natural communicator – incredibly warm and full of knowledge and enthusiasm about the natural world, and he ended up as co-presenter.

When the long-running show finally ended in the mid-eighties, Terry was instrumental in the creation of CBBC's groundbreaking *Really Wild Show*. The BAFTA winning mix of studio-based, largely adlibbed animal items and humorous features, revolved around Terry's irreverent, larger-than-life character, and the show spearheaded a new era of less stuffy BBC Children's programmes.

Perhaps unusually for a celebrity, it gave him great pleasure to be recognised, spending whole evenings sharing his passion about animals with a rapt audience of complete strangers down the pub.

When, after seven years, he left the *Really Wild Show*, he made no secret of his disappointment that he never quite achieved the same level of fame again. But his place as a TV legend had been secured among the generations who had been inspired by his genuine respect for animals and nature. On the sad news of his death, tributes poured in from fellow professionals and the general public.

TV presenter Phillip Schofield remembered Terry as: "a delightful man and passionate naturalist." Zoo-keeper Paul Paterson said: "Nature has indeed lost another magical fellow creature. He was the real genuine article." Viewer Sarah from Hampshire wrote simply: "Rest in peace in a ring of bright water, Mr Nutkins x"

The world has lost a huge, inspirational character but his spirit shines brightly in the natural world he loved so much.

Peter Wiltshire 1931-2012

Paul R. Jackson

Former BBC Children's producer/director/writer on classics like *Play School* and *Vision On*, Peter Wiltshire passed away after a fall at home which led to a fatal stroke. He died on 27th October 2012 aged 81.

Peter joined the BBC in 1953 as a cameraman and during this time he contributed to the "Packi the Elephant" stories that Tony Hart drew for *Blue Peter* (1959-61). He later worked again with this inspirational artist and presenter when he directed *Vision On* (1969-70). Peter began writing scripts for *Play School* in 1964 and, in September 1965, started an attachment with the Children's Department. He left the BBC staff in 1983 and worked as a freelance for two years, writing stories for the *Buttons* children's comic.

His nephew, Steve Gorman, said Peter had enjoyed a wonderful life and that he had told him that the highlight of his later life, since retirement, was attending the launch of my book – which he and his family had very much enjoyed - at BAFTA and seeing again so many old colleagues. This was lovely to hear and nice that he had the chance to see them at such a happy occasion. His funeral took place on 15th November at All Saints Church, Beeston, Norfolk, with both the *Play School* and *Play Away* themes played at the end of the service.

Contributors

Cary Bazalgette

Cary Bazalgette was Head of Education at the British Film Institute from 1999 to 2006. She has written and edited a number of teaching resources and books about moving-image media education and has given presentations on this topic in 24 different countries around the world. Her most recent book (as editor) is *Teaching Media in Primary Schools* (Sage 2010) and her most recent teaching resource is Animagine (Film and Video Workshop 2011). She blogs about her current research at http://toddlersandtv.blogspot.co.uk/

Beakus

Beakus is an animation production company based in London that brings together a wealth of award-winning talent. We create top-notch animation for CBeebies, CBBC, Nickelodeon and publishers like Nosy Crow. We work across 2D, 3D and Stop Motion with a diverse roster of designer/directors – Steve Smith, Gergely Wootsch, Leo Bridle, Mr Binns, Sarah Orenstein, and Leigh Hodgkinson. Our work includes the series *Numtums* (25x5-minutes) for CBeebies, seasonal idents (7x1-minute) for CBeebies Presentation, *Totally Rubbish* for Dot To Dot and CBBC, Weetabix Spoonsize bumpers for Nickelodeon, and an app for Nosy Crow, 'Animal SnApp: Farm'. Website www.beakus.com

David Buckingham

David Buckingham is a Professor of Media and Communications at Loughborough University, UK, and a Visiting Professor at the Norwegian Centre for Child Research. His work focuses on children and young people's interactions with electronic media, and on media education. His most recent research has focused on issues such as consumption and 'sexualisation'; the role of the internet in promoting civic participation; and the teaching of media literacy in primary and secondary schools. Latest books include *Beyond Technology: Children's Learning in the Age of Digital Culture* (2007); *Global Children, Global Media; Migration, Media and Childhood* (2007); *Video Cultures: Media Technology and Everyday Creativity* (2009); and *The Material Child: Growing Up in Consumer Culture* (2011). Contact: d.buckingham@lboro.ac.uk.

Michael Carrington

As Chief Content Officer for Cartoon Network Europe, Michael Carrington is responsible for the strategic direction of Turner's children's programming within Europe, the Middle East and Africa (EMEA). He leads the development & production unit, programme acquisitions, and oversees several business areas, including franchise management, programme compliance, and central creative services. He also acts as liaison across Turner International on all matters relating to content and channel branding. Throughout his career, Michael has worked for some of the world's premier broadcast companies, including Network Ten Australia, Discovery Communications Europe, and the BBC. Michael is a member of the British Academy of Film and Television Arts, the International Academy of Television Arts and Sciences, an ardent champion of animation, and regularly speaks at industry events.

GREG CHILDS

Greg Childs worked for 25 years at the BBC, as a director, producer and executive-producer of children's programmes. He created the first Children's BBC websites and, as Head of Children's Digital, developed and launched the children's channels: CBBC and CBeebies. On leaving the BBC in 2004, Greg became a consultant working with producers on digital strategies and broadcasters on channel launches. He is the co-creator and Editorial Director of the Children's Media Conference, a Head of Studies at the German Akademie Für Kindermedien, and Director of the Children's Media Foundation. Greg was made a Fellow of the RSA in 2010 in recognition of his contribution to children's rights and culture.

TONY COLLINGWOOD

Tony is Producer/Writer/Director with Collingwood O'Hare Productions which he formed back in 1988 with Chris O'Hare. Since then, he has been writing and directing animated shows through his company for broadcasters and distributors worldwide. His credits include *Dennis the Menace*, *Harry and his Bucketful of Dinosaurs*, and BAFTA award-winning shows, *Yoko! Jakamoko! Toto!* and *The Secret Show*. He is currently producing the Dr. Seuss series, *The Cat in the Hat Knows a Lot About That!* for CITV, PBS and other broadcasters worldwide. He has been a long standing member of the PACT Children's Committee and is also a board member of Directors UK

MARSHALL CORWIN

Marshall is an Emmy-winning TV and radio producer who has produced BBC flagship shows from *Tomorrow's World* to *Newsround*. He has made films in many extreme and dangerous environments, and he created and produced the internationally acclaimed *Serious* ... an environmental adventure series. Seen in 150 countries, it won an unprecedented four BAFTAs and three RTS awards. He co-authored *Nutkins on Pets* with close friend, animal presenter Terry Nutkins, and his most recent book, *Extreme Survival: An Adventurer's Guide to the World's Most Dangerous Places*, was shortlisted for a Royal Society Science Book Prize. He is currently a director of production company BlackandWhiteTV.

PETER FLAMMAN

Pete Flamman is Senior Vice President, Chief Operating Officer at Turner Broadcasting EMEA. He also holds the post of Managing Director of Turner Kids EMEA giving him overall editorial and commercial responsibility for Turner's kids activities in EMEA.

Between 2008-12, Pete was General Manager Northern Europe, responsible for Turner's Entertainment Businesses in: UK and Eire; Central and Eastern Europe; Germany, Austria and Switzerland; Nordics; and Benelux.

As Vice President Business Development, Pete played a key role in Turner's growth. Pete's first project at Turner was the launch of Boomerang UK in May 2000 and he has been involved in the launch of dozens of new channels and services, including Boing on Italian DTT and the roll out of TNT in EMEA.

Pete joined Turner in March 2000 after working at Spectrum, a boutique strategy consultancy.

JOE GODWIN

Joe Godwin, Director of BBC Children's, is responsible for all of the BBC's services for children – the CBBC and CBeebies channels and their websites, including the CBeebies Radio online service and the CBeebies Grown-ups site. After reading History at Manchester University, Joe joined the BBC in 1986, working at BBC Southampton in regional news. In 1989, he joined BBC Children's as a trainee assistant producer, studio director and producer on shows such as *Blue Peter*, *Going Live* and *Record Breakers*. From 1997 to 2000 he was Editor of Children's Presentation. In 2000 he moved to Nickelodeon UK, holding a number of posts including Head of Original Production and VP Interactive Director. Joe returned to the BBC in 2005 as Head of Children's Entertainment. In 2009 Joe took up his current post as Director of BBC Children's, and in 2011 led the move of the entire Children's department to its new home at MediaCityUK in Salford. Joe is a member of the BAFTA Children's Committee, The Advisory Panel on Children's Viewing of the British Board of Film Classification, and represents the BBC on The UK Council for Child Internet Safety.

EVGENIA GOLUBEVA

Evgenia is a freelance illustrator, writer and animation director for children's media, based in London. She studied Directing and Writing for Animation in St. Petersburg University of Cinema and TV in Russia, and Writing for Children in London. She has about five years of experience working across different platforms (children's TV series, apps, books). Visit her website for more information, showreel and portfolio: www.evgeniagolubeva.com

BETH HEWITT

Beth works across a range of Postgraduate and Undergraduate Creative Media programmes at University of Salford, where she is senior lecturer. She leads the MA in Documentary Production and MA in Wildlife Documentary, and, drawing upon many years work at ITV Granada and BBC North, and her wealth of industry networks, went on to create and develop the MA in Children's Digital Media Production. Much of her work at the University is focused around industry engagement and for three years she was Co-director of Exposures Film Festival in collaboration with Cornerhouse, Manchester. Beth also project manages media festivals and events across the Creative Media department such as the One World Media Festival last year.

ANNA HOME, OBE

Anna joined BBC radio in 1960 and started in Children's Television in 1964 where she worked as a researcher, then Director, Producer and Executive Producer, latterly specialising in Children's Drama where she started *Grange Hill*. From 1981 to 1986 she worked at the ITV company TVS where she was Deputy Director of Programmes. In 1986 she returned to the BBC as Head of Children's programmes: she revived the Sunday teatime classic dramas and one of her last decisions before retiring was to commission *Teletubbies*. After retiring from the BBC, Anna was Chief Executive of the Children's Film & Television Foundation until it merged into CMF in 2012. Anna has won many awards including a BAFTA lifetime achievement award. She was the first chair of the BAFTA Children's Committee, has chaired both the EBU Children's and Youth Working Group and the Prix Jeunesse International Advisory Board. Anna was the Chair of the Save Kids' TV Campaign Executive Committee and the Showcomotion Children's Media Conference, and now chairs the Board and Advisory Committee of the Children's Media Conference, and is a Board member of Screen South. Anna is Chair of the CMF Board and a Founding Patron of the organisation.

OLI HYATT

Oli Hyatt has been Creative Director at Blue-Zoo for thirteen years, helping it thrive through difficult times for the animation industry; Blue-Zoo won "Production company of the year" at BAFTA this year. His most recent show, *Olive the Ostrich*, is a huge hit on Nick Jr, and has been sold right around the world. He is the director of Alphablocks Limited, the company behind CBeebies phonics show *Alphablocks*, as well as being the Chair of Animation UK. The former Young Businessman of the Year, former Young Animator of the Year, former Young Director of the Year, has realised he's too old to enter all these awards so is now focusing on bringing a slate of his new programmes to children everywhere.

PAUL R. JACKSON

Paul is author of *Here's a House – a Celebration of Play School* (Volumes One and Two). His love of children's television started as a viewer in the late 1960s with favourites including *Play School* and *Camberwick Green*. He worked for the BBC from 1984 and in 1993 was asked to lead the new Duty Office team at ITV's Carlton TV where he remained until being made redundant in 2001. From 2002 to 2009, Paul worked in hospitality, organising major conferences and weddings at venues, including Leeds Castle and the Holiday Inn. Since 1998 he has worked as a freelance stage manager on nearly 150 award shows and since 2010 has worked as a Porter at Albany. Paul's books are available direct from Kaleidoscope Publishing:

http://www.kaleidoscopepublishing.co.uk/books-playschool1.html
http://www.kaleidoscopepublishing.co.uk/books-playschool2.html

JAYNE KIRKHAM

Jayne has spent her life working with and writing for all sorts of young people including those with special educational needs and young offenders. Her writing is full of warmth and heart, and puts the 'art' back into 'fart'. While TV is her first love, most recently she has worked on *Ajani's Great Ape Adventures*: a pan-African conservation film project and her current commission is also for a feature based on the award winning Gussie novels. Believing that good children's media is of vital importance not just for a child's wellbeing but also for the country's, Jayne is applying that warmth and heart to Politics. And yes, she's putting the 'art' back too.

NICK MACKIE

Nick Mackie is an animation director and illustrator. He has won an RTS award, BBC Talent Animation, and his short films have been in competition at various international festivals. In 2012 he published his debut children's novel *Edison and the Dinosaur Zoo* and is writing a second. He worked for many years as a creative at Aardman Animations, 4:2:2 and Picasso Pictures. Nick is currently freelance and developing a project of illustrated preschool books. www.dinosaurzoo.co.uk Website: www.shufti.co.uk

PAUL MADDEN

Paul Madden was part of an original team of four at the formation of Channel 4 in 1981, when founding chief executive Sir Jeremy Isaacs asked him to take charge of proposals for animation. Through commissioning Aardman and a host of emerging talent, Madden put Channel 4 on the map as an innovative and imaginative broadcaster of animation. His commission of John Coates's wordless animation of Raymond Briggs's *The Snowman* has an enduring global legacy.

GREG McLEOD

Greg McLeod is an award winning illustrator, animator and director. Greg has a distinctive hand-drawn style and has worked on a wide range of projects including animation, illustration, exhibitions and book covers. Greg is a BAFTA winner, has won a Webby, won an Association of Illustrators Gold Award and won a variety of awards at film festivals. Website: http://www.brothersmcleod.co.uk/

MÁIRE MESSENGER DAVIES

Máire Messenger Davies is Professor of Media Studies at the University of Ulster, Coleraine, Northern Ireland. She's also a Visiting Professor at the University of Glamorgan, in Cardiff. A former newspaper, magazine and radio journalist, including a spell as Deputy Editor of *Mother & Baby* magazine, she has a lifelong interest in the relationship between children and the media, especially television; this includes bringing up four children of her own. She has degrees in English Literature (BA) and Psychology (PhD) and has taught in universities on both sides of the Atlantic. She is the author of *Television is Good for Your Kids* (Hilary Shipman 1989/2001), *Fake, Fact and Fantasy: Children's Understanding of TV Reality,* (Laurence Erlbaum 1997), and, more recently, *Children, Media and Culture* (Open University Press 2010).

OFCOM

Ofcom, established by the Communications Act 2003, is the independent regulator and competition authority for the UK communications industries. Details of the full range of Ofcom's activities are available on the website www.ofcom.org.uk. For further information regarding Ofcom's contribution to this volume, please contact Alison Preston, Head of Media Literacy Research. Alison.Preston@ofcom.org.uk

REBECCA PARRY

Rebecca joined the University of Leeds in Dec 2011 as a lecturer in Childhood Studies. Formerly a teacher in secondary schools, she has also worked as a cinema educator and as a children's film festival director. She developed a media production project, Cube, which gave young people the opportunity to collaboratively create media such as magazines, websites and films in order to express opinions as well as gain creative skills. Her doctoral research focused on the impact of film and film production on children's understandings of narrative and she has recently been awarded First Light funding to undertake further research into young people's contemporary film production with the Institute of Education and the British Film Institute (BFI). She has taught on EdD and MA courses at the University of Sheffield, and has written an MA module entitled 'Children, Film and Literacy', a partnership between BFI and the University of Sheffield.

Lydia Plowman

Lydia Plowman is Professor of Education and Technology at the University of Edinburgh. The focus of her research has moved away from the compulsory years of schooling and formal learning environments to families and the home. This, in turn, has led to a shift in emphasis away from desktop computers to diverse domestic and leisure technologies. She explores different ways of enabling young children to be active participants in research, as well as involving family members in such a way that we can gain insights into their practices, values and attitudes.

John Potter

John is a Senior Lecturer in Education and New Media at the London Knowledge Lab in the Department of Culture, Communication and Media at the Institute of Education, University of London. His research and publications are in the fields of: digital video production by young learners (the focus of his doctoral research); the use of social software and online networks for publication and learning; media education, new literacies, creative activity and learner agency; and the changing nature of teaching and learning in response to the pervasive use in wider culture of media technologies in formal and informal settings. He is the author of *Digital Media and Learner Identity: The new curatorship* (Published in Dec 2012 by Palgrave MacMillan).

Sioned Wyn Roberts

Sioned Wyn Roberts is S4C's Content Commissioner responsible for Children's, Learning and Digital. She is a programme maker with 22 years experience of producing children's content for television, radio and, more recently, interactive digital media. At S4C Sioned is responsible for all children's programmes on the channel: preschool brand Cyw and children's strand Stwnsh. She is also developing the Learning slate for children and adults and is working with S4C colleagues and external partners to develop new digital content for the channel. Sioned started her career in the media in 1990 when she joined the BBC and has worked as a researcher, producer, director and series producer. Sioned was a Senior Producer in the Education and Learning Department at BBC Wales for six years from 2001 to 2006 and led several award-winning multi-platform campaigns such as *Come Clean, B*ll*cks,* and pan-Celtic Language Learning project *Colin and Cumberland.* Sioned joined the independent sector in 2006 and was Creative Director at Griffilms animation company for two years. From 2008 to 2012, she worked as an independent producer on children's projects such as CBeebies interactive project *Alphablocks* and CBBC series *Stuck on Sheep Mountain.* Sioned was recently a member of the task and finish group looking at *Digital Materials in Education* for the Welsh Government. Before joining the media, Sioned was a History teacher for eight years. She has two children who consume digital media voraciously.

Jeanette Steemers

Jeanette Steemers is Professor of Media and Communications at the University of Westminster. Before becoming an academic she worked as an industry analyst for CIT Research and HIT Entertainment. Her book publications include *Creating Preschool Television* (2010), *Regaining the Initiative for Public Service Media* (2012, co-editor), *Media in Europe Today* (2011, co-editor), *European Television Industries* (2005, co-author), *Selling Television: British Television in the Global Marketplace* (2004) and *Changing Channels* (1998, editor). She has written many articles on policy and economic issues affecting children's media.

Melanie Stokes

Melanie set up Kindle Entertainment with Anne Brogan in 2007. Since then she has exec-produced *Jinx*, a live-action comedy series for CBBC; *Dustbin Baby*, an International Emmy-winning drama for BBC One starring Dakota Blue Richards and Juliet Stevenson; *Some Dogs Bite*, a feature-length drama for BBC Three starring Thomas Brodie-Sangster; and mini-series *Treasure Island* for Sky One starring Eddie Izzard, Donald Sutherland and Elijah Wood. Melanie has also exec-produced Series One and Two of *Leonardo*, an action-adventure series that she co-created with Pia Ashberry for CBBC; and mini-series *The Life & Adventures of Nick Nickleby* for BBC, a modern-day retelling of Charles Dickens's classic tale. She is currently exec-producing an animated preschool series, *Dinopaws*, for CBeebies and YTV, Canada.

Jeremy Swan

Jeremy Swan joined RTE when it started in 1960, and in 1966 went to work for Granada armed with a recipe for paella and a Spanish dictionary: leaving-Ireland presents from his granny. From floor managing *Coronation Street* he went to the BBC where he became a producer in BBC Children's. After a time as a director on *Jackanory*, he inherited *Rentaghost*, written by Bob Block. Bob then wrote a series for Clive Dunn, *Grandad*. Jeremy went from the BBC to TVS to direct *Fraggle Rock* for the Jim Henson Organisation, and, on returning to the BBC, Anna Home sent him to Melbourne to work on *Round the Twist* for the Australian Children's Foundation. *Sooty* invited Jeremy to direct him, Sweep and Soo for ITV. He currently works as a painter (pictures, not walls) and as a playwright, based in London.

Alexandra Swann

Alexandra's PhD research into the politics and economics of preschool children's television was undertaken at the University of Ulster and funded by the Department of Employment and Learning. She is currently a freelance researcher based in Northern Ireland, with particular interests in children's television, young children's internet use, and the experiences of children growing up in post-conflict societies.

Jo Twist

Dr Jo Twist took the role of CEO of UKIE in January 2012. Dr Twist comes from Channel 4 as Commissioning Editor for Education where she commissioned Digital Emmy-winning *Battlefront II*, a stable of free browser and iOS games, including *Sweatshop*, *Nomnation* and *International Racing Squirrels*, as well as social media projects. Previous positions include Multi-platform Commissioner for BBC Entertainment & Switch, BBC Three Multi-platform Channel Editor and in a former life was a technology reporter for BBC News. With a background in digital media, education, creative technology and youth culture, Jo brings a wealth of experience in all aspects of interactive entertainment including media, technical innovation and creativity, commercial and political issues.

An Vrombaut

An Vrombaut was born in Belgium and moved to London to study animation at the RCA. Her graduation film, *Little Wolf*, went on to win numerous international awards. After graduating, An's love of animals lead her to create *64 Zoo Lane*. Four series have been produced and broadcast on BBC/CBeebies since 2000. Another TV series, *Florrie's Dragons*, is based on her *Dear Dragon* books. An has written fourteen picture books including *Smile, Crocodile, Smile*, which was a winner at the Nottingham Children's Book Award. She is currently developing her short film *The Tie*.

www.vrombaut.co.uk

Lynn Whitaker

Lynn Whitaker is based at the Centre for Cultural Policy Research, University of Glasgow. Lynn's research concentrates on UK children's media production culture; her PhD, funded as an AHRC collaborative doctoral award, was a production study of BBC Scotland's Children's department as both a 'small nation' production facility and a BBC 'centre of excellence'. At postdoctoral level Lynn has carried out audience research for Disney and for IZI, thus allowing her insight into every stage of the production cycle from development to consumption. Lynn's next interest is to look at how the new tax breaks – and contingent cultural test – impact on games development and animation in Scotland. Prior to undertaking postgraduate study in Film and TV studies (MLitt) that led to her PhD, Lynn was a qualified teacher in Scottish secondary education (English and Drama) for over ten years and holds undergraduate degrees in Law as well as in Arts: at HE level she has taught across law, literature and childhood studies as well as more typical 'media' based disciplines. It is the nexus of policy, production and audience concerns that continues to drive Lynn's research. And lots of Earl Grey Tea. yearbook@thechildrensmediafoundation.org